Is Jesus Revealed in the Old Testament?
(A Study of The Old Testament High Priest)

By

Adrian Harris

Is Jesus Revealed in the Old Testament?
A Study of the Old Testament High Priest

Adrian Harris (C) January, 2010

ISBN 978-0-9790625-9-9

All rights reserved. No part of this publication may be reproduced, stored in a retrieval system,
or transmitted in any form or by any means-for example, electronic, photocopy, recording-without the prior written permission of the author.
The only exception is brief quotations in printed reviews.

Scripture Quotations are from the King James Version of the Bible

Additional books by Newburgh Press
may be found on www.newburghseminary.com
Books are available through Amazon.com
BarnesandNoble.com and other
bookdealers

Newburgh Press
Newburgh, Indiana

"To my loving wife, Lucie, I dedicate this book as a token of my love."

Table of Contents

Preface   7

Chapter 1   9

Chapter 2   17

Chapter 3   23

Chapter 4   65

Chapter 5   73

Chapter 6   81

Chapter 7   87

Bibliography   89

PREFACE

My purpose in writing this book is to give a comprehensive study of God's redemptive plan as outlined in the Old Testament High Priest. It is my earnest desire for the study to encourage and enable diligent students of the Word to become actively engaged in researching the truths related in the typology of the high priest.

Grateful recognition is also extended to Mrs. Sue Gerringer for her help in typing the final manuscript. It is with a deep sense of gratitude that I offer this dissertation to the Newburgh Seminary and every Christian who desires to study the great truths of the Bible.

My deepest gratitude goes to my Lord who made the redemptive plan of salvation possible through His atoning blood. To God be the Glory!

Chapter 1

INTRODUCTION

The Bible contains many types and metaphors. It conveys a panoramic view mixed with various illustrations depicting the truths related in the Word of God. Jesus consistently revealed truths through the medium of parables, which illustrate metaphors. The word, "parable," is derived from the Greek word, "paraballo, "composed of the preposition "para" meaning "beside" and the verb "ballo" meaning "to cast." [1] A parable would therefore consist of two objects used in comparison to relate or cast a truth in teaching or preaching.

This study will involve a critical analysis of the typology of the High Priest related to Christ, the great High Priest. It will prove beyond any reasonable doubt that the High Priest in the Old Testament Levitical order, describes, points to, illustrates and types the Lord Jesus Christ, the great High Priest, as a mediator between God and man. It will demonstrate a comparison between the two and will conclusively prove the type of antitypes found in the Bible, both New and Old Testaments, to be Biblically sound. The study will prove that in Christ the Law of God was fulfilled. "The Christian church is built on Old Testament foundations." The Book of Hebrews declares, (4:14):[2]

---

[1] Merrill C. Tenney, The Zondervan Pictorial Bible Dictionary Grand Rapids, Michigan: Zondervan Publishing Hours, 1970), p .621

[2] Charles F. Pfeiffer, The Epistle to the Hebrews, (Chicago, Illinois: Moody Press, 1962) p. 40

.... we have a great High Priest."[3] Christ, the great High Priest, has passed beyond this world to the heavens and is now enthroned at the right hand of the Father. His exalted position is the ground for the Christian confidence. When the High Priest in the Tabernacle entered the Holy of Holies, he could do so only once a year. But, Christ, the great High Priest, is now seated in the Holy of Holies in the presence of the Father, at His right Hand.

Christ, the exalted High Priest, is in no sense remote from His children. He knows the nature of humanity because at one point in the history of the world, He became flesh or man. A characteristic of man, or human nature, is temptation. Christ was tempted in every point that man has been tempted and yet without sin. The Savior, the great High Priest, experienced human temptation, such as lust of the flesh, lust of the eyes and the pride of life. The result of the fall to temptation by Adam was physical and spiritual death, but the victory of Christ over temptation resulted in spiritual life or a spiritual resurrection.

Christ has the ability and is willing to intercede for His children. Because of His assured love, His children may approach Him with an unfailing confidence. The approaching assurance that Christians possess is one of the great characteristics of the New Covenant.[4] The Old Testament Israelite was unable to enter the Holy Place or the Holy of Holies, the throne room of God. The Israelite was made to stand afar off because of the righteous and holy presence of God. Through Christ, the great High Priest, the believer may approach God at any time or any place.

---

[3] Holy Bible, Authorized King James Version. The Scofield Reference Edition. (New York, N.Y. Oxford University Press, 1945)

[4] Charles F. Pfeiffer, The Epistle to the Hebrews, (Chicago, Illinois: Moody Press, 1962) p. 40

The righteousness of Christ has been imputed into every believer, which makes it possible for the believer to approach the holy and righteous God. The believer now has the confidence of intercession because of the accepted atonement at the mercy seat of God in glory.

    The Levitical priesthood as well as Christ, the great High Priest, had to meet the prerequisites and qualifications before acceptance as the High Priest. The Levitical priesthood differs from the priesthood of Christ, but both had to be accepted by God. A great deal of truth has already been discussed on the humanity of Christ. He was God and man at the same time. He was human and Divine or a dual being. He possessed the characteristics of man as well as the characteristics of God. Christ was chosen among those whom He came to this world to represent before the unapproachable God. It is a Biblical truth that man brought sin into the world, and it is necessary for deliverance and salvation to come by man. Jesus was the God-man, and is seated at the right hand of God, as the God-man. Jesus, the Son of God, became the Son of Man, that man, the son of man, might become the sons of God.

Jesus was appointed to act on behalf of man in relation to God. A prophet addresses man as God's spokesman, whereas the priest comes to God with a prayer and offering on behalf of man.[5] Jesus undertook both of these ministries.

    The sacrifices of Christ were like that of the Levitical order. However, the word "sacrifice" implies the shedding of the blood of an innocent victim. Merrill Tenny States:

> "The motives actuating the offerer may be varied, worthy or unworthy, and may express faith, repentance, adoration, or all of these together; but the main purpose

---

[5] Charles F. Pfeiffer, <u>The Epistle to the Hebrews,</u> (Chicago, Illinois: Moody Press, 1962) p. 41

of the sacrifice is to please the deity and to secure His favor."[6]

The words and works of the Son of God formed a prelude to His offering Himself to God for the atonement of the sins of the world. A priest must have a sacrifice to offer and Christ offered Himself, as that needed sacrifice. The word "sacrifice" according to the Greek implies that Christ met the specifications for being the perfect sacrifice. It also implies that Jesus, who was God, offered Himself willingly and unreservingly to His Father as the total, complete and all-sufficient sacrifice for the sins of the world.[7]

In contrast to Christ, the Levitical priest had to make atonement for his sins as well as the people's sins. The priest had been tempted and yielded to that temptation, but Christ never once sinned nor yielded to sin. This results in the implication that the Levitical Priest cannot serve as an effectual mediator. He had personal guilt that required atonement and for this reason help must come from another. "The whole sacrificial system foretold of the redemptive work of Christ."[8]

Christ, a Priest after the Order of Melchizedek

The only time Melchizedek is mentioned in the Old Testament is in the

Book of Genesis. He is portrayed as a character of ancient Biblical history. Lot, Abraham's nephew, had journeyed into

---

[6] Merrill C. Tenny, The Zondervan Pictorial Bible Dictionary, (Grand Rapids, Michigan: Zondervan Publishing House 1970) p. 737
[7] George R. Berry, The Interlinear Greek-English New Testament (Grand Rapids, Michigan: Zondervan Publishing House, 1974) p. 860
[8] Oliver B. Greene, Our Saviour, (Greenville, South Carolina: The Gospel Hour, Inc., 1969) p. 30

the wicked city of Sodom and became involved in an active political life. The kings of the East formed a coalition and defeated the city of Sodom as well as its allies. Lot was taken captive by the kings of the East and Abraham felt the responsibility of his nephew resting upon his shoulders. Abraham gathered his household together and journeyed to the far North Country and surprised the enemy and rescued Lot.

Upon a successful campaign, Abraham stopped at Salem where he paid tithes to the priest-king of the city, Melchizedek. Melchizedek blessed Abraham with the words, "Blessed be Abram of the most high God, possessor of heaven and earth; and blessed be the most high God, which hath delivered thine enemies into thy hand." (Genesis 14: 19-20)[9]

Who was this Melchizedek? He is mentioned as the ruler of Salem. He is said to be the priest of El Elyon, "the most high God." Abraham recognized Melchizedek as a true priest and one that truly worshipped God in the idolatrous times. It was thrilling for Abraham to observe people who were worshipping the true and living God, that were not a part of the family of patriarchs. The thought comes to mind that there were men of God in position with power that were totally sold out and dedicated to the "most high God."

The book of Hebrews shows that Melchizedek was a Priest-King, which is a suitable type of Christ. Melchizedek is a compound name. The Hebrew word "melech" means, "king," and "zedek" is the usual word for "righteousness." The compound form means, "king of righteousness."[10]

Melchizedek was also melech ("king") of Salem, a name related in meaning to the common Hebrew word

---

[9] Holy Bible, Authorized King James Version, Pilgrim Edition, (New York, N.Y.: Oxford University Press 1952)

[10] A. Marshall, The Interlinear Greek-English New Testament (Grand Rapids, Michigan: Zondervan Publishing House, 1972) p. 861

"shalom" (Arabic, salam), "peace."[11] Melchizedek, the man who blessed Abraham had a double role—king of peace and king of righteousness.

These attributes of Melchizedek present a two-fold picture of Christ. Righteousness is an attribute of God. Man is totally lost in sin and has no righteousness of his own. The Gospel of Christ proclaims that what man cannot do for himself, God has done. He has provided a righteousness, in the Person of His Son, Jesus Christ. He bore the sins of the world upon His body and because of His atoning work; every believer has the imputed righteousness of Christ dwelling in their hearts. This is the righteousness that God demanded for salvation apart from the works of man. Because of His imputed righteousness into the heart of every believer, a child of God may approach the throne of Grace at any time.

Melchizedek was also a king of peace. The Bible refers to Christ as, "the Prince of Peace." Jesus declared that He brought peace and was going to leave peace with us. The believer has the promise of perfect peace. This peace is presented in the Epistle of the Romans as a result of the death and resurrection of Jesus:

> "Who was delivered for our offences, and was raised again for our justification. Therefore being justified by faith, we have peace with God, through our Lord Jesus Christ." (Romans 4:25-5:1)[12]

The word "shalom" speaks of well-being. The peace of Christ marks the end to all hostilities. The sinner is out of harmony with his fellow man as well as God. Peace restores this harmony. Peace restores fellowship and relationship. A lost man is the child of the devil, but when he receives Christ into his heart, he becomes a child of God, thereby restoring

---

[11] James Strong, Strong's Exhaustive Concordance, (Grand Rapids, Michigan: AP and A Publishing Company). p. 3197

[12] Holy Bible, Authorized King James Version, The Schofield Reference Edition. (New York, N.Y.; Oxford University Press, 1945). p. 1196

the relationship lost in the sin of Adam and Eve. The peace that Christ gives is an inner peace that comforts the heart and mind when problems and difficulties arise.

The person who studies Melchizedek, finds that he was without father or mother or descent. He had neither beginning of days nor end of life. The reader will also find that the man who did not have the proper genealogy could not function as a priest. The Book of Hebrews tells us that the priesthood of Melchizedek was not dependent upon his family relationship. This pictures Christ as the One, "whose goings forth have been from old, from everlasting" (Micah 5:1). Jesus proclaimed in the Book of Revelation, "I am He that liveth and was dead; and behold, I am alive forevermore." There was no beginning to Christ and neither will there be an end to Him. He is from "everlasting to everlasting."

The Superiority of Christ's Priesthood

Psalm 110 portrays the emphatic priesthood of Melchizedek. In the Levitical order there were many priests. This became necessary because the priests were mortal and would eventually die. The succession was arranged so that someone would officiate at the altar at all times. The Priesthood of Christ is not so, in that it remains eternally. The Bible informs the believer that Christ, "ever liveth to make intercession for them." The work of Christ was not only for the atonement of sins, but also for the continuing ministry as the believer's advocate.

The Old Testament Priest was to offer a daily succession of sacrifices. The Priest sacrificed offerings for the people and for themselves. The Priests themselves were sinful men, although they were God's children. Christ, the Great High Priest, is contrasted with the Old Testament priest in that He was the spotless Priest. The Priests made continuous sacrifices while Christ made one; He offered Himself. No one can add to this all-sufficient sacrifice that was accepted by God as the propitiation for the sins of the world. The superiority of Christ's Priesthood can be summed up in four dramatic phrases: (1) He was perfect; (2) His priesthood is eternal; (3) His priesthood is sacred; (4) He is the Person, of God's Son.[13]

From the brief introduction, the reader may establish the importance of the high priest in the tabernacle and his position as related to Christ. The dramatic position gives magnitude to the superiority of the Priesthood of Christ. Christ's priesthood is with an everlasting reign and service. The world and other so-called priests of different religions have challenged his effectiveness, but the name of Christ and His eternal reign continues in the heavenlies to make intercession for the children of God. His answer to prayers has proved His effectiveness. The lives that have been transformed are living epistles and examples of His power to save and mediate between God and man.

---

[13] Oliver B. Greene, The Epistle of Paul, the Apostle to the Hebrews, (Greenville, South Carolina: The Gospel Hour Inc. 1969) p. 270

Chapter 2

THE PRIESTHOOD

The Priesthood, the tabernacle and its vessels all point to one main theme or subject. The tabernacle would have been of no use if it were not for the vessels. The tabernacle could have been completely constructed and all the vessels in place, but there would be no services if it were not for the priest.

Each part demands the other. It connects like a chain with its many links. If one part is missing the chain becomes two parts, thus causing an incomplete chain.

The priest that offered the gifts served as an example of the shadow of heavenly things. God admonished Moses on the mount to make the tabernacle by the pattern that God had revealed to him.[14]

The priests were divided into three main groups as seen from the Old and New Testaments:

(1) Priests. This refers to the members of the Aaronic family. The claim for this office was sonship. The work of these priests was to minister in holy things.

(2) High Priests. Aaron was the first high priest. He was succeeded by his son, and so on, generation after generation. Only one high priest held office at a time. A new priest did not succeed until the death of the officiating high priest. History reveals that there were eighty high priests between the office of Aaron and Christ.

(3) Great High Priest. There was only one Great High Priest and he remains in his heavenly position at the present. He was and is the Lord Jesus Christ. He was a

---

[14] Henry W. Soltau. The Tabernacle, (Fincastle, Virginia: Scripture Truth Book Company). p. 187

priest after the order of Melchizedek. He did not come from the Aaronic order, nor from the tribe of Levi. He did not receive His Priesthood from anyone and neither will He pass it on to anyone. He reigns eternally because of His unchanging ministry and endless life.[15]

The priesthood was not given to every person. The Bible gives a detailed account of the priestly requirements. The requirements are not given to show the Christian minister, but rather the importance and the type of the High Priest in relation to Christ. The requirements intended to cast a shadow of the qualities and character, and office of the Great High Priest, the Lord Jesus Christ. In the light of what has been discussed, consider the requirements and qualifications of the office of the High Priest: (1) the Priest was required to be physically perfect. This was true because it represented perfect humanity, which was found in Jesus Christ. He could not be blind or lame because the Priest had to signify that Christ was without spot or blemish.[16] The Word was fulfilled and the end result tells the story, "there was no guile found in His mouth." He was required to be without spot or blemish so that Israel might know what type of Priest-King to expect. (2) The priest was required to be properly and purely mated. The reader thinks of Christ not being married, but soon He will to His bride, the Church. He has chosen the Church as a chaste virgin. The Bible reveals that the wife of the priest could not be divorced, not a vile offender, nor an unclean thing. The Bible informs the reader that, "Christ loved the Church and gave Himself for it." He wants His Church to be one of complete faithfulness. The Church will be presented without spot,

---

[15] Charles W. Slemming, These Are the Garments, (Chicago, Illinois: Moody Press, 1955) p. 9-10

[16] J. A. Seiss, The Gospel in Leviticus, (Grand Rapids, Michigan: Zondervan Publishing House) p. 333

wrinkle or blemish.[17] The requirements of the priest's wife relate to the reader the importance of the church and her role in the work of the Lord. (3) The children of the priest must be pure. A transgression of his children degraded him from his position. The nature of the office of a Pastor is very noticeable by the world. The wrongs that his children acquire were readily laid to this charge. A disobedient child resulted in the loss of power by the priest as well as a Pastor today. It points to the fact that everything proceeding from the union of Christ is pure and holy. (4) The priest was required to be holy. They could not defile themselves by having contact with the dead, unclean things, by irreverence toward holy things, or by eating improper food. They constantly must observe the laws. They were to devote themselves to their office as anointed men of God.[18] They were to be separated from all forbidden things. The prominent factor in the life of Christ as the mediator and Great High Priest is His holiness. He had to be perfectly pure and holy to be acceptable to God. Christ is observed from every aspect of life and constantly, He is revealed as the harmless, undefiled Son of God and mediator between God and Man.[19] (5) The priest must be chosen from the tribe of Levi. Christ did not come from this tribe because He was the priest after the order of Melchizedek. "Christ was taken from among men of our flesh and bone."[20] (6) The priest also had to be a man of knowledge. This pointed to the perfect knowledge of Jesus Christ as the Great High Priest.

---

[17] Benjamin Keach, Preaching from the Types and Metaphors of the Bible, (Grand Rapids, Michigan: Kregel Publications, 1972) p. 980

[18] J. A. Seiss, The Gospel in Leviticus, (Grand Rapids, Michigan: Zondervan Publishing House)

[19] Sammuel Ridout, Lectures on the Tabernacle, (New York, N. Y.: Loizeaux Brothers Inc., 1973) p. 506

[20] Benjamin Keach, Preaching from the Types and Metaphors of the Bible, (Grand Rapids, Michigan: Kregel Publications, 1972) p. 982

The priest was also a type of Christ in the execution of his office:

(1) The priest was totally responsible for killing the sacrifices. This signified the voluntary action of Christ, by laying down His life for us. No one could take this away from Him. (2) The priest had to offer the sacrifice to God and sprinkle the blood of the sacrifice on the altar. No one could offer the sacrifice but the priest, thereby causing everyone to come to the priest as the mediator between God and the sinning Israelite. This represents Christ offering His own blood as the sacrifice for the sins of the world and no one can come to the Father except through Christ, the Great High Priest, who has offered the total and complete sacrifice. No one was able to take away the sin but Christ. (3) The priest was responsible for reaching the people with the knowledge he possessed. The knowledge that the priest conveyed came from his lips. Christ is figured as the Great Doctor and Teacher of the mind of God. Christ spoke the words of everlasting life. (4) The priests were to preserve oil for the lights, for incense, for daily meat offering and for the anointing oil, signifying that Christ is the Preserver of all grace.[21]

There were some tasks performed by the priest that were given in certain time sequences:

(1) He was to dress the holy lamps, morning and evening, before the Lord, to keep the lights from going out. This typifies Christ preserving the light of His Gospel from all foes and demons that continuously try to hinder and consume the light of the Gospel. (2) The priest had to make shew-bread weekly and set it on the table and take away the old bread. This typifies Christ as setting Himself before the world in His continued ministry of the Word. He strengthens His children and brings forth freshness every day. (3) The priest, in the Day of Atonement, which was yearly, went into

---

[21] Ibid. p. 982

the holy of holies with blood to make expiation for his sin, for his house, and for all the people. This typifies Christ opening the sanctuary of heaven, offering His blood for the atonement on our behalf, and before God makes intercession for every believer.[22] The priest continually judged the highest controversies. He judged between the clean and unclean, putting away one and receiving the other into the congregation. This signifies that Christ is the judge and the supreme one over all controversies, and His word alone can decide the case, who is clean, and who is unclean, who to put out and who to take in.[23]

---

[22] Benjamin Keach, Preaching from the Types and Metaphors of the Bible, (Grand Rapids, Michigan: Kregel Publications, 1972) p. 982
[23] Ibid. p.982

Chapter 3

THE GARMENTS OF THE PRIESTS
The Garments for Glory and Beauty

"And Thou shalt make holy garments for Aaron and thy brother for glory and for beauty.
"And Thou shalt speak unto all that are wise hearted, whom I have filled with the spirit of wisdom, that they may make Aaron's garments to consecrate him, that he may minister unto me in the priest's office.
"And these are the garments which they shall make; a breastplate, and an ephod, and a robe, and a broidered coat, a mitre, and a girdle: and they shall make holy garments for Aaron thy brother, and his sons, that he may minister unto me in the priest's office." (Exodus 28: 2-4)

The garments for glory and beauty are directed to be made for the use in the office of the Priest. They are made that Aaron might be consecrated. They dignified his person, which he did not possess himself. This was used to magnify the Person and office of the everlasting Son of God. His obedience to the Father by his death upon the tree proved Him to be worthy of the highest exaltation at the right hand of the Father. Christ, the Great High Priest, dignifies the office of the priest whereas the office added dignity to Aaron.[24]
There are many contrasts drawn between Christ and Aaron. Aaron was the High Priest while he lived, but Christ was called from the dead by the resurrection, to be the High Priest. Aaron was taken from among men. He had and was

---

[24] Henry W. Soltau, The Tabernacle, (Fincastle, Virginia: Scripture Truth Book Company) p. 191

compassed with their infirmities, like they were, and needed to offer a sacrifice for his sins as well as theirs.

Christ was not taken from among men. He was raised from the dead as the Son of God. There was no sin in Him and no trace of mortality. Christ was tempted in all points as man was and yet without sin. His life, sorrow and temptation perfected Him for the Ministry of the Priesthood.

Some of the Priests in the house of Levi were cut off from the Priesthood because they were made without an oath. But Christ was made a Priest with an oath from the Father: "The Lord sware, and will not repent." The Priesthood of Aaron continued from generation to generation, but the priesthood of Christ cannot be passed on because He lives forever.

Aaron was made a priest after the flesh, from the tribe of Levi. Christ became the Great High Priest after the power of His endless life and victory over death.[25]

The Ephod and the Robe of the Ephod

"And they shall take gold, and blue, and purple, and scarlet, and fine linen.

"And they shall make the ephod of gold, of blue, and of purple, of scarlet,

and fine twined linen, with cunning work." (Exodus 28: 5,6)

"And of the blue, and purple, and the scarlet, they made cloths of service, to do service in the holy place, and made the holy garments for Aaron; as the Lord commanded Moses.

---

[25]Laurance T. Chambers, Tabernacle Studies Illustrated, (Grand Rapids, Michigan: Zondervan Publishing House, 1958) p. 106.

"And he made the ephod of gold, blue, and purple, and scarlet, and fine twined linen." (Exodus 39: 1-2)

There are two materials specified for the making of the ephod—gold and fine twined linen. The colors specified are blue, purple and scarlet, interlaced by the gold. The beauty of the gold was blended into every part giving the ephod a firmness and brilliancy, to the whole fiber.

The ephod was the outermost garment worn over the blue robe. One part of the ephod covered the front and the other the back reaching nearly to the knees. The ephod was very costly and magnificent. The principal feature of the ephod was that the onyx gems rested on the priest's shoulders.[26]

Notice that the term "robe" is used for the first time in the Book of Exodus chapter thirty-eight. The robe is to be distinguished from the coat. The coat is used specifically for a purpose of covering. The robe is worn as a symbol of authority and office. The robe carries the idea of dignity and royalty. This points to the robe that Christ wore when He was about to be crucified, "And they stripped Him, and put on Him a scarlet robe...." (Matthew 37:28)[27]

The robe of the ephod was seamless which contributed to the fact that it was not possible for man to rend it. A hole was placed in the top of the robe so that the head of the priest could pass through. The hole had a neck band attached that was bound to the strength of habergeon. A habergeon is an armored plate, which God commanded Moses to make.

The face that the robe was woven in one piece shows the Eternal Deity, Divine Personage, and matchless grace of the Lord Jesus Christ.

---

[26] W. G. Moorehead, The Tabernacle, (Grand Rapids, Michigan: Kregel Publications, 1966) p. 96
[27] Charles W. Slemming, These are the Garments, (Chicago, Illinois: Moody Press, 1955) p. .41.

Notice that the robe of the ephod was made of blue. Blue is the typical color for GRACE. The Bible states, "Grace and truth came by Jesus Christ." (John 1:17) The blue reminds the reader of the blue sky that seemingly brings cheerfulness. It shows the goodness and grace of the Lord Jesus Christ.[28]

The hem of the garment displayed pomegranates and golden bells alternating all the way round. The pomegranates were made of blue, purple and scarlet. These were used as a pad to keep the pomegranates and the golden bells from clashing against each other, preventing noise or disruption. The pomegranates present a picture of fruitfulness to us. The two spies brought back pomegranates to show the fruitfulness of the land. The pomegranates are typified as the fruit of peace, giving a picture of Christ as the fruit of God that has brought peace into the heart of every believer. Between the pomegranates were the golden bells. They tell us of the gospel of peace. Each bell has a distinct mellow ring, but blended together into a beautiful melody. The gospel of Christ brings a melody into the life of everyone who has appropriated that gospel of peace into their hearts. The High Priest did not wear the bells on the Day of Atonement when he went into the holy of holies to offer the blood because it was a day of humility.[29] On this day the priest wore plain white garments of linen. The priest wore the robe every other day in the year, when he ministered in the Holy Place.[30] It was here that the sound of the bells could be heard, because man was not permitted to enter any part of the tabernacle except the court. While the priest moved, the people knew he was still

---

[28] I.M. Haldeman, The Tabernacle, Priesthood and Offerings, (Westwood, New Jersey: Fleming H. Revell Company) p. 281.
[29] M.R. Dehaan, The Tabernacle, (Grand Rapids, Michigan: Zondervan Publishing House, 1969). p. 180
[30] Henry E. Soltau, The Holy Vessels and Furniture, (Grand Rapids, Michigan: Kregel Publications). p. 84

alive. The believer can know that Christ is still alive, by the bells of Joy that Christ brings to their hearts. The believer knows that Christ lives because He is making intercession for them. All of these picture Christ as the eternal, endless, Son of God.

The Ephod Girdle

"It shall have two shoulder pieces thereof joined at the two edges thereof, and so it shall be joined together.
"And the curious girdle of the ephod, which is upon it, shall be of the same, according to the work thereof: even of gold, of blue, and purple, and scarlet, and fine twined linen." (Exodus 38:7,8)

"They made shoulder pieces for it, to couple it together. And the curious girdle of his ephod, that was upon it, was of the same, according to the work thereof: of gold, blue, and purple, and scarlet, and fine twined linen: as the Lord commanded Moses." (Exodus 39:4,5)

The ephod was made of two pieces joined together and bound to the high priest by a girdle or belt.

The word "curious" here refers to the curious embroidery. It seems to have been a belt, to bind the ephod to the high priest. The materials and the color of the girdle are of significant importance.

The gold gave the girdle strength as well as giving it glory and brilliance. Gold is the emblem of Eternal Deity, which speaks of the Godhead. Gold was a metal that stood the test of time. Nothing will alter the gold. After being buried thousands of years, the gold deposits have never deteriorated. Gold may be melted and remelted without the loss of oxidation. The gold pictures of Christ are endless and eternal.

Previous discussion has already shown that blue typifies the sky, heaven or Divinity. Gold and blue, side by side, represents Deity and Divinity. Blue reminds the believer of God's handiwork in the heavens. "The heavens, therefore, tell of infinite space, but Christ is infinitely greater."[31]

Blue and scarlet can stand in great contrast to each other. Many times, purple can blend the two together. You look up to see the blue of the sky and you must look down to see the red of the earth. Scarlet therefore, shows Christ stepping down from heaven's glory, humbling Himself and becoming obedient unto death. The scarlet represents the humanity of Christ. The blue representing the Divinity and the scarlet representing humanity shows the dual nature of God---the God-man. The contrast between the two colors represent sin and causes them not to blend.

Purple stands as the intermediate color. Christ came to man and in man's likeness to bring man back to the likeness of God. As blue and scarlet represent Christ as the God-man, the purple represents Him as the Mediator between God and man. A mediator is a person bringing two contending parties together in an agreement. Christ was God, who became man, that He might bring man back to God. "For there is one God and one Mediator between God and man, the Man Christ Jesus." (I Timothy 2:5)

With the colors possessing great spiritual truths, one must look at the background upon which the colors were placed. The fine twined linen represents the essence of His righteousness, apart from which He could have not become Mediator and Priest. Man has no righteousness of his own and through Christ

---

[31] Charles W. Slemming, These are the Garments (Chicago, Illinois: Moody Press, 1955) p. 50

man receives the imputed righteousness of God into his heart. The righteous--ness of Christ satisfied the demands of the Law of God.[32]

The curious girdle was neither loose nor attached but one with the ephod. The girdle "so connected the ephod with the person who wore it as to impart to him the virtues it contained."[33] The robe with all the spiritual truths related in color and material—His Righteousness, His Divinity, His Humanity, His
Mediatorship and His Peace; are bound to Him because they are a part of Him. The girdle, therefore, imparted the virtues of the robe to the priest. The believer is to be so bound up in Christ that His character becomes a part of us.

The Onyx-Stones, Ouches and Chains

"And thou shalt take two onyx stones, and engrave on them the names of the children of Israel.
'Six of their names on one stone, and the other six names of the rest on the other stone, according to their birth.
'With the work of an engraver in stone, like the engraving of a signet, shalt thou engrave the two stones with the names of the children of Israel: thou shalt make them to be set in ouches of gold.
"And thou shalt put the two stones upon the shoulders of the ephod for stones of memorial unto the children of Israel: and Aaron shall bear their names before the Lord upon two shoulders for a memorial.
"And thou shalt make ouches of gold;

---

[32] Charles W. Slemming, These are the Garments (Chicago, Illinois: Moody Press, 1955) p. 53
[33] Charles W.Slemming, These are the Graments (Chicago, Illinois: Moody Press, 1955) p. 54, 55

"And two chains of pure gold at the ends; of wreathen work shalt thou make them, and fasten the wreathen chains to the ouches." (Exodus 38:9-14)

"And they wrought onyx-stones enclosed in ouches of gold, graven as signets are graven, with the names of the children of Israel.
"And he put them on the shoulders of the ephod, that they should be stones for a memorial to the children of Israel; as the Lord Commanded Moses." (Exodus 39:6,7)

God gave Moses a list of things to be brought and the onyx-stones was mentioned. The names of the children of Israel according to their birth were on each stone, six on each. They were enclosed in the settings of gold or called the ouches. "The onyx-stones in their settings were fastened upon the shoulder pieces of the ephod, so as to rest upon the shoulders of the High Priest." [34] Aaron was to bear the names of the children of Israel upon his shoulders as a memorial before the Lord.

The Breastplate

"And thou shalt make the breastplate of judgment with cunning work; after the work of the ephod thou shalt make it; of gold, of blue, and of purple, and of scarlet, and of fine twined linen, shalt thou make it.
"Foursquare it shall be being doubled; a span shall be the length thereof, and a span shall be the breadth thereof.

---

[34] Henry W. Soltau, The Tabernacle (Fincastle, Virginia: Scripture Truth Book Company) p. 201

"And thou shalt set in it setting of stones, even four rows of stones; the first row shall be a sardius, a topaz, and a carbuncle: this shall be the first row.

"And the second row shall be an emerald, a sapphire, and a diamond.

"And the third row a ligure, an agate, and an amethyst.

And the fourth row a beryl, and an onyx, and jasper: they shall be set in gold in their inclosing.

"And the stones shall be with the names of the children of Israel, twelve, according to their names, like the engravings of a signet; every one with his name shall they be according to the twelve tribes.

"And thou shalt make upon the breastplate chains at the ends of wreathen work of pure gold.

"And thou shalt make upon the breastplate two rings of gold, and shalt put the two rings on the two ends of the breastplate.

"And thou shalt put the two-wreathen chains of gold in the two rings, which are on the ends of the breastplate.

"And the other two ends of the two-wreathen chains thou shalt fasten in the two ouches, and put them on the shoulder pieces of the ephod before it.

"And thou shalt make two rings of gold, and thou shalt put them upon the two ends of the breastplate in the border thereof, which is in the side of the ephod inward.

"And two other rings of gold thou shalt make, and shalt put them on the two sides of the ephod underneath, toward the forepart thereof, over against the other coupling thereof, above the curious girdle of the ephod.

"And they shall bind the breastplate by the rings thereof unto the rings of the ephod with lace of blue, that it may be above the curious girdle of the ephod, and that the breastplate be not loosed from the ephod.

"And Aaron shall bear the names of the children of Israel in the breastplate of judgment upon his heart, when he goeth in unto the holy place, for a memorial before the Lord continual." (Exodus 28:15-29)

"And he made the breastplate of cunning work, like the work of the   ephod; of gold, blue, and purple, and scarlet, and fine twined linen.

It was foursquare; they made the breastplate double: a span was the length thereof, and a span the breadth thereof, being doubled.

"And they set in it four rows of stones: the first row was a sardius, a topaz and a carbuncle: this was the first row.

"And the second row, an emerald, a sapphire, and a diamond.

"And the third row, a ligure, an agate, and an amethyst.

"And the fourth row, a beryl, and onyx, and jasper: they were enclosed in ouches of gold in their inclosing.

"And the stones were according to the names of the children of Israel, twelve, according to their names, like the engravings of a signet, everyone with his name, according to the twelve tribes.

"And they made upon the breastplate chains at the ends, of wreathen work of pure gold.

"And they made two ouches of gold, and two gold rings; and put the two rings in the two ends of the breastplate.

"And the two ends of the two-wreathen chains of gold in the two rings on the ends of the breastplate.

"And they made two rings of gold, and put them on the two ends of the breastplate, upon the border of it, which was on the side of the ephod inward.

"And they made two other golden rings, and put them on the two sides of the ephod underneath, toward the forepart of it, over against the other coupling thereof, above the curious girdle of the ephod.

"And they did bind the breastplate by his rings unto the rings of the ephod with a lace of blue, that it might be above the curious girdle of the ephod, "And that the breastplate might not be loosed from the ephod: as the Lord commanded Moses." (Exodus 39:8-21)

The word "breastplate" means an ornament. The Septuagint translates it by the Greek word, logeion, or oracle.[35]

The High Priest stood before God with the breastplate on to represent Israel in a double capacity. The stones that rested upon his shoulders gave the names of the children of Israel according to their birth.

1. On the onyx on the left shoulder
   A. Gad
   B. Asher
   C. Issachar
   D. Zebulun
   E. Joseph
   F. Benjamin

2. On the onyx on the right shoulder
   A. Reuben
   B. Simeon
   C. Levi
   D. Judah

---

[35] Henry W. Soltau, The Tabernacle (Fincastle, Virginia: Scripture Truth Book Company) p. 204

E. Dan
F. Naphtali

The stones on the breastplate were arranged in four rows of three. The names were engraved on them according to the tribes.

The first row:
    Carbuncle   Topaz   Sardius
    Zebulun   Issachar Judah

The second row:
    Diamond   Sapphire Emerald
    Gad   Simeon   Reuben

The third row:
    Amethyst   Agate   Ligure
    Benjamin   Manasseh Ephraim

The fourth row:
    Jasper   Onyx   Beryl
    Naphtali   Asher   Dan

Because the Hebrew language is written from right to left the stones would probably be arranged as written.[36]

Many times the breastplate is called the "breastplate of judgment." The only purpose of the breastplate was to be a repository for the Urim and the Thummin. The breastplate was doubled so that the Urim and the Thummin fitted easily into the small pouch. The breastplate was foursquare just as the Tabernacle.[37] Being foursquare means that it is a geometrical figure, which has equal measurements. It

---

[36] Henry W. Soltau, The Tabernacle (Fincastle, Virginia: Scripture Truth Book Company) p. 206

[37] A. B. Simpson, Christ in the Tabernacle (Harrisburg, Pennsylvania: Christian Publications Inc.) p. 6

represents and speaks of solidity, balance and equality. The breastplate was nine inches square and covered the entire breast of the high priest. The breast is a symbol of affection and love and this represents the love Christ has toward the believer.

There were four chains attached to the breastplate itself while two held secure the ephod. The four rings in the breastplate were placed in each corner. Wreathen chains of gold coming from the upper rings linked the breastplate to the shoulder- stones. The chains and laces were gold and blue, picturing the Deity and the Grace of Deity. God in heaven demands holiness. This characteristic was found in Christ, accepted by God, and the two golden chains linked them together. Gad demanded holiness, while man below needed Grace and Mercy. "Christ reached down and gave them to man and so the laces of blue linked man to Christ."[38]

Later man was given the ribbon of grace to wear. This is attested to the story found in the Book of Numbers, chapter fifteen. Later in the chapter man was found gathering sticks on the Sabbath day, breaking the commandment of God. God weighed the matter and decided to be merciful and commanded the children of Israel to make fringes on the borders of their garments through the generations, and to put a ribbon of blue upon those fringes. This was a reminder to the children of Israel that God is a merciful and a covenant keeping God. This must have been what Luke was referring to when he told of the woman with an issue of blood touching the hem of the garment of Christ and being made whole instantly.

The breastplate contained twelve stones, each one representing a tribe of the children of Israel. The first application presented of the stones in the breastplate is that of being near to God and in His presence. The High Priest

---

[38]Charles W. Slemming, These are the Garments (Chicago, Illinois; Moody Press, 1955) p. 59

wore the breastplate next to his heart and breast, which indicates being near to God and His loving bosom.

Also notice that the stones were set in their closings by the gold. It has already been stated that gold represents the Eternal Godhead and that the breastplate with its many colors pictures Christ. This indicates and sets forth the truth that the believers are set into Christ by God the Father, the Eternal Godhead.[39]

The reader must also observe the stones and their order. They were placed in order. God is consistent in order. He formed a plan before the foundation of the world and His plan is being carried out perfectly and in order. The believer can see the majestic power of God in the creation of the world, the universe and man. The order of the stones indicates that the Eternal God has a place in His will for every man. Man must find God's will for his individual life and proceed to carry it out until fulfilled completely. Paul knew the Lord had a plan for his life when he was struck to the ground by the risen, glorified Lord. He found God's will for his life and continued in it until the time of his departure. Paul had run a good race, and fought the fight and kept the faith and his life was snuffed out by the acts of an ungodly man. The believer's life must be one of superior trials and temptations. Christ did not promise the easiest life in the world, but He did promise to send the comforting power of the Holy Spirit in the believer's heart.

Another impression of the breastplate was that no two stones are alike. What does this picture or represent? It presents a picture of the believers and their different personalities. Although believers belong to the same body, no two believers are alike. Notice the stones were placed on one breastplate. This illustrates the oneness of the body of Christ. Believers are different, but they are made into one

---

[39]Charles W. Slemming, These are the Garments (Chicago, Illinois; Moody Press, 1955) p. 60

body. There are many members in the body of Christ, but there is only one body, which exists.

The stones were called "precious stones." Every believer---poor, rich, black, white, blind or lame---is precious in the sight of God. The Bible instructs the believer to be no respecter of persons. Why? Because God never has been nor will be a respecter of persons. "The rain falls on the just and the unjust." The believer has the promise that God has as much love for him as anyone in the world. The reason the believer is precious to God, is because of the great price that was paid to purchase their redemption. Christ did not die to be a propitiation for a limited group of people, but everyone. It has been declared, "If a man dies in his sin and goes to hell, he will go there with his sins paid in full, but refused the payment for those sins.

The reader will discover that the names of the children of Israel were engraved on the stones, representing the whole of Israel. This picture presents the child of God being engraved in the heart of God, as the spiritual Israel. The stones were set in the breastplate and it was linked to the ephod with the curious girdle. It was impossible to remove one of the stones without removing the glory of the robe. The robe was only removed once a year when the High Priest laid it aside to put on a white, plain robe to enter the holy of holies to offer a blood sacrifice, sprinkled on the Mercy seat seven times. This was the Day of Atonement. God accepted the blood, and the priest came out and assured the people of God's forgiveness. He then proceeded to put on the garments of glory and beauty and continued his daily administration.

Jesus in time past, laid aside the garments of his glory and put on the plain robes of humanity, stepping down to the earth and man for the explicit purpose of offering, not just a sacrifice, but Himself as the all-sufficient sacrifice for the sins of the world. After His resurrection, He ascended into heaven passing beyond the veil of the sky, presented

Himself to the Father with his nail pierced hands and feet to be totally received and accepted by the Father with the great heavenly reunion. He proceeded to put on the garments of glory and beauty which He had laid aside, and then sat down at the right hand of the Father, never to remove those garments of glory again.[40]

The Stones of the Breastplate

Each of the stones on the breastplate was different. The names of the children of Israel were written upon these stones in a categorical sequence. The study will reveal that the different stones were chosen for each specific name. In each of the stones a definite connection relating to the name, person and nature was seen. The connections are to be found between their birth, their father's blessing and the tribal blessing of Moses.

Sardius

The color of the Sardius was red. The name Judah was inscribed on the stone representing praise, glory and worship of God.

The red color of the Sardius is the color of wine. It also represents the color of blood. Judah was the object of praise according to the blessing of Jacob. It would be filled with joy, praise and glory. The land would be filled with vineyards, making the wine bountiful.

Judah also washed his garments in wine, and his clothes in the blood of grapes. The vine of the grapes referred to the pursuits of Judah in the field. The blood of the grapes was used for the cleansing of the garments and clothes. The clothes that were worn everyday received a purging as well as the robes of glory. The believer finds

---

[40] Charles W. Slemming, These are the Garments (Chicago, Illinois: Moody Press, 1955) p. 65

need of the blood of Christ for His cleansing power, to clean them from everyday sins that taint their lives. The blood of Christ preserves the heart of the believer and our priestly robes of purity, which enables the child of God to have access to the presence of God.[41]

The wine presented a picture of joy and merriment. The believer has a "joy unspeakable and full of glory." The presence and saving power of Christ fills the heart of God's people with joy and happiness.

"His eyes shall be red with wine, and his teeth white with milk." Many people spend their days filled with drunkenness. They drink away their lives with intoxicating beverages to determine that tomorrow shall be as today. Instead of using the poison of intoxicating wine, the believer's teeth will be white with milk. The saints of God will be as newborn babes. They shall desire the sincere milk of the Word. The milk of God's Word will flow from their mouths and the testimony of Christ will go forth as the remedy for the sins of the world.

The red color of the stone connects with the name of Judah. The lord Jesus was the first to utter praise to God. In his death and His shedding of His blood. May the believer give praise also to God for the blood of Christ that has cleansed their lives from all sin? The beauty of the Sardius shines forth the song of thanksgiving to the Savior. May His name reign forever as proclaimed?

<u>Topaz</u>

This is a gem known in modern days. It is a precious stone of a rich yellow luster. The name of Issachar was engraved on the stone meaning, "hath given hire or

---

[41]Henry W. Soltau, The Tabernacle (Fincastle, Virginia: Scripture Truth Book Company) p. 210

recompense."[42] The word "reward" is found in the name of Issachar. God will reward everyone, whether good or evil, secret or open. He will also reward the saints for their faith in Him. The word "recompense" means a giving back in return for. God will give in return what we have given Him.

The Lord Jesus is the true Issachar. He trusted in His Father, and has been faithfully delivered. He has finished His task for the Father and glorified His precious name on earth. Christ received His reward when He was glorified by the Father and received the glory He had with the Father before the world existed. His being obedient unto death resulted in His exaltation at the right hand of the Father, and gave Him a name that is above every name.

It is said of Issachar: "Issachar is a strong ass, couching down between burdens. And he saw that the rest was good, and the land that it was pleasant; and bowed his shoulder to bear, and became a servant unto tribute." (Genesis 29: 14,15)

The idea conveyed that Issachar anticipated the goodness of the rest, and the pleasantness of the land, resolved, for the sake of reward, to bow his shoulder to bear, and become subject to servitude. Remember that the Israelites despised the land and questioned God as to where they would be able to enter it.[43] Because of their disbelief, their carcasses fell in the wilderness. God has set before the believer, rest. Jesus said, "Come unto me, all ye that labor and are heavy laden, and I will give you rest. Take my yoke upon you, and learn of me; for I am meek and lowly in heart: and ye shall find rest unto your souls. For my yoke is easy and my burden is light." (Matthew 11:28-30) Everyday the believer experiences a Sabbath; a day of rest in their souls.

---

[42]Henry W. Soltau, The Tabernacle (Fincastle, Virginia: Scripture Truth Book company) p. 212

[43]Henry W. Soltau, The Tabernacle (Fincastle, Virginia: Scripture Truth Book Company) p. 213

Carbuncle

The name of Zebulun was inscribed on the Carbuncle stone. The Hebrew word for Carbuncle is "Bareqeth" meaning "glittering," and it is evidently derived from a Hebrew root used sometimes for "lightning" or "flashing." [44] This may picture Zebulun as a lighthouse with its flashing light warning the mariner of dangers, or welcoming the storm-tossed traveler to seek the refuge of haven. It was also a haven for ships. There were probably docking facilities for the landing and unlanding of the vessels. The blessing of Zebulon makes known the fact that the nation enjoyed the abundance of the sea.[45]

What a picture of the lost sinner docking into the harbor of God's love and forgiving grace. God welcomes the weary, worn, tearstained traveler of this storm-tossed world into a haven of rest, not just as a place of rest, but where they can unload their sorrows, burdens, and discharge their sins and then receive joy, peace, and happiness.[46] Jesus was the light of the world as long as He was in the world, but He informed the believers before going back to heaven, that when He left, Christians would be the light of the world. While He walked and lived on the earth, He pointed people to the Father. Christians are to be a lighthouse warning of the dangers and perils of rejecting Jesus Christ as their Lord and Saviour. Not only are the believers to warn of the dangers of sin, but relate the forgiving, mercy and grace of God. Believers should point the lost to Christ, the refuge of God, as a place of safety and rest.

---

[44] Charles W. Slemming, These are the Garments (Chicago, Illinois: Moody Press, 1955) p. 85
[45] Arno, C. Gaebelein, The Annotated Bible Vol. 1 (Neptune, New Jersey: Loizeaux Brothers, Inc., 1970) p. 439
[46] Charles W. Slemming, These are the Garments (Chicago, Illinois: Moody Press, 1955) p. 85-86

Emerald

The name of Reuben was found inscribed on the precious emerald. Like the rest, Reuben was a faltering man, but still precious in the sight of God. The emerald is a sea green color. The name of Ruben was very significant on the stone because it represented him being as unstable as the restless sea. He was unstable, but yet on the Breastplate of stability. Many times the believer is unstable in their ways, but yet still saved and safe in the arms of the Savior.[47]

The firstborn of Leah was Reuben. Upon his birth she declared, "Surely the Lord hath looked upon my affliction; and accordingly she called his name Reuben." Jacob looked upon the child as being unstable as the sea. This was a deep reflection in fact to the instability of his father. May the Lord help every believer to become stable in the Word of God and not make the mistakes that Reuben encountered.

Sapphire

"The English word Sapphire is evidently taken from the Hebrew word "Sappeer" which is derived from a verb signifying "to scratch or polish," and also means, "to cut off or divide."[48] The Sapphire is the second hardest stone in the world. It is very interesting to notice that the name of Simeon was inscribed on the stone and later became the foundation for his name.

This precious stone was a pure deep blue. According to the Elders in Exodus, this formed the pavement under the

---

[47] Henry W. Soltau, The Tabernacle (Fincastle, Virginia: Scripture Truth Book Company) p. 216
[48] Charles W. Slemming, These are the Garments (Chicago, Illinois: Moody Press, 1955) p. 97

feet of the God of Israel. Ezekiel gazed on the throne of glory, which had the appearance of a sapphire stone.

This precious stone displayed the same color of the ephod-blue. This presents the body of heaven in its clearness. God dwells in the heaven, where His throne of glory is displayed.

The blue also speaks of love. God is love. Love fills the heart for His church, and that love was manifested when Christ gave Himself a ransom for the sins of the world.

The love of God is shown in His rebuking and chastening hand. He declares, "those whom I love, I chasten and rebuke."

One must notice that Simeon was the second born son of Leah. In naming her two sons, Leah brought two senses into operation---"seeing" and "hearing." The Bible reminds the believer that the Lord constantly has His eyes of omnipresence on the righteous as well as hearing our petitions made unto Him.

Diamond

"Diamond, in our English Lexicon, is the same word as 'adamant' and adamant means 'impenetrable hardness,' hardness that cannot be broken."[49] The Diamond referred to in the Bible is derived from the Hebrew root meaning "to break in pieces or bruise." This stone can break or scratch all others. From observing diamond cutters one may see that the stone is used to cut glass and other precious stones. The stone can make an indelible mark without harming itself. This was true of Gad.

Gad was the son of Zilpah, the handmaiden of Leah. The name "Gad" means "a troop." The history of Israel will

---

[49]Charles W. Slemming, These are the Garments (Chicago, Illinois: Moody Press, 1955) p. 102.

reveal that the tribe of Gad was of great military strength. The Bible describes the great power of the tribe as, "valiant men, men able to bear buckler and sword, and to shoot with bow, and skillful in war." (I Chron. 5:18)

The Church of Jesus Christ is a troop of believers. Many times believers become pressed down with the problems and burdens of this life. The god of the world seems to be the victor. The believer must realize that Christ has already won the victory and that he is not fighting for victory, but rather walking in it. Every believer who wishes to be an overcomer must overcome themselves. As the Diamond represents "hardness" may the saints of God be hard to move from the faith, but at the same time be soft enough for the hand of God to mold and shape our lives.

Ligure

The name of Ephriam was written upon this stone. Very little is known about the stone and commentators differ as to what modern day stone it may be. Most of them suggest it to be the modern jacinth or yellow jargoon. "Flinders Petrie identifies it with the yellow agate."[50] Because of its uncertainty one seems to refrain from making a spiritual application.

Ephriam was the second son of Asenath, the wife of Joseph. The word "Ephraim" means, "doubly fruitful." Before the death of Jacob, Joseph brought his two sons at the bedside and asked his father to bless them. Joseph wittingly switched their hands and Ephraim received the first blessing. When Joseph tried to correct Jacob, his father assured him that his action was deliberate. From that day on, one will read about Ephraim, and Manasseh, not

---

[50]Charles W. Slemming, These are the Garments (Chicago, Illinois: Moody Press, 1955) p. 108

Manasseh and Ephraim. The incident lead to both of the sons becoming the name of two tribes of Israel. This way they both found a place on the Breastplate as tribes, but never on the shoulder-stones as sons by birth.

One writer has stated in a spiritual application, "Believers are the blessing that God has given to Christ in the land of His affliction."[51]

__Agate__

The name of Manasseh was inscribed on the agate and set into the Breastplate. The agate is a semi-translucent compound mineral. When the agate is properly cut and polished, it produces variegated stones. The agate is much harder than steel, and is sometimes used in scientific instruments instead of steel. The original stones were found at Achates in Sicily. The first appearance of the stone is rough and unattractive. The cutting process brings the beauty and the colors to an interesting display.[52]

The mention of the stone occurs only twice in the Book of Exodus where the stones of the breastplate are enumerated. It has already been discussed about the name of Manasseh being engraved on the stone, but now one can take a look at what Manasseh means and who he was in relation to Joseph. The name "Manasseh" means "forgetfulness." Joseph called his elder son Manasseh because the Lord had said to Joseph, "He hath made me to forget all my toil, and all my father's house." The order of the two sons names were reversed in the arrangement of the tribes, because Ephraim, the younger son, received the blessing of Jacob over Manasseh.

---

[51] Henry W. Soltau, The Tabernacle (Fincastle, Virginia: Scripture Truth Book Company) p. 222

[52] Charles W. Slemming, These are the Garments (Chicago, Illinois: Moody Press, 1955) p. 113

The picture of the meaning of Manasseh displays the forgiving and for-getting nature of God. When a sinner received Christ as Lord and Saviour, God blots out all of their sins, to remember them again no more. "He cast their sins in the sea of forgetfulness." It is not a very wise practice to forget. Forgetfulness in the business world leads to bankruptcy. Forgetfulness of your wife's birthday will lead to a broken-hearted woman. When man forgets, it is a sign of weakness, but when God forgets it is a sign of power. He can and does forget the sins of people who have trusted Him by faith.[53]

The Christian must also be forgetful in certain areas. Paul said, "Forgetting those things which are behind, and reaching forth unto those things which are before, I press toward the mark for the prize of the high calling of God in Christ Jesus." (Phil. 3:13-14) The Christian must never let the things of the old nature and the past discourage him from pressing forward toward greater things. God has forgotten the believer's past and so should he.

Amethyst

"It is agreed that the common amethyst, properly called amethystine quartz, is meant. This is rock crystal colored purple by manganese and iron. The Oriental amethyst is a much rarer gem, composed of violet corundum (oxide of aluminum) – in short, a purple sapphire. The name of the amethyst is derived from its supposed property, no doubt associated with its wine-like color, of acting as a preventive of intoxication."[54]

---

[53] Henry W. Soltau, The Tabernacle (Fincastle, Virginia: Scripture Truth Book Company) p. 224.
[54] Charles W. Slemming, These are the Garments (Chicago, Illinois: Moody Press, 1955) p. 120.

The English Dictionary says: "A bluish-violet kind of quartz, formerly supposed to prevent intoxication (Gk. a-methustos, not drunken; from methuein, be drunk)."[55]

The stone was very hard. This applies to the tribe of Benjamin. Many times they were headstrong and warlike in character. One time in the history of the tribe a battle resulted because a Levite abused and killed his wife. The tribe faced 40,000 men to their 26,700 men. The battle was a gruesome war. The Book of Judges summed the entire battle as intoxication.

The surrounding of the birth of Benjamin was a sad situation. The favorite wife of Jacob was Rachel but she was in great distress because she was barren. On many occasions she sought to force the issue. She made the first suggestion to give her handmaiden to Jacob hoping that she would have a son and thereby adopt him. On one occasion she cried unto Jacob, "Give me children, or else I die." In time God did give her a son called Joseph, but it cost her her life. God gave her the child, but she died in childbirth.

In the anguish of her childbirth she called and named her son, Benoni, meaning, "the son of my sorrow." After her death Jacob changed his name to Benjamin, meaning, "the son of my right hand."

The title, "Son of Sorrow," presents a picture of Christ as the Man of Sorrows. Jesus put down the royal robes of glory and came to this sin cursed earth to die a cruel, vicarious death. He became the "Man of Sorrows," because of the suffering and shamed He endured. He was despised of men and treated in the manner of a dog. Yes, Jesus became the "Man of Sorrows," to bring peace and joy to the heart of every believer. The title, "Son of my right hand," presents Christ as being at the Father's right hand. Notice that the name, Benjamin, was given by Jacob, his father. Remember that Christ too was named by his Father and has

---

[55]Ibid., p. 120

been "given a name that is above every name." Benjamin was loved so by his father because it cost the life of his wife to have him. The believer must remember that they are "Benjamins" in the sight of God because of what it cost Him to attain our new spiritual life.[56] Jesus, who was the Son of His Father's right hand, became the "Son of sorrows" that lost mankind might become the sons of God.

Beryl

The name of Dan was inscribed on the beryl. Which was very hard. The name Beryl means, "to break or subdue."[57] Ezekiel referred to this stone when he spoke of the swift, powerful chariots and wheels, which was seen by the prophet. The Song of Solomon describes the hands of the Bridegroom, which were set in beryl.

The impatience of Rachel caused her to give the handmaiden over to Jacob to gain a son by proxy. This revealed a lack of trust in God. She then took the child of Bilhah and said, "God hath judged me," and called his name Dan, which means, "Judge."[58]

The reader will also notice that the Bible informs them that Dan was to judge his people as one of the tribes. It did not mean that Dan was going to judge all the tribes, but rather judge his people: not as a superior, but as an equal. He would not be judging other, but himself. This message holds true to the believer. The believers are to judge themselves so that they will not be judged. Self-judgment keeps the believer in God's standards rather than their own.

---

[56]Charles W. Slemming, These are the Garments (Chicago, Illinois: Moody Press, 1955) p. 117.
[57]Walter Lewis Wilson, Wilson Dictionary of Bible Types (Grand Rapids, Michigan: W. B. Eerdman's Publishing Co., 1965) p. 54
[58]Charles W. Slemming, These are the Garments (Chicago, Illinois: Moody Press, 1955) p.122.

The name for beryl indicates that the believer and their lives are to be broken and remolded by the hand of God. The believer's life is to be subdued to willful submission to the will of God.

Onyx

The Bible speaks of the onyx as being precious and brilliant. This presents difficulty in detecting what type of stone it refers to today. The onyx stone today is neither brilliant nor precious. "According to Robertson the Hebrew word "Shoh-ham" is derived from an unused root signifying "to shine with the luster of fire" and "a flashing forth of splendor."[59]

This was the second child of Zilpah and adopted by Leah, who also named him. As she took the child in her arms she declared, "Happy am I, for the daughters will call me blessed." (Genesis 30:12-13) She then named the child Asher meaning "Happy" or "Blessed." The Bible informs the believer of true forgiveness. The man who is forgiven is blessed or happy. The reason people can be happy when their sins are forgiven is because the guilt of their sin has been washed away in the blood of Christ. The believer stands in the sight of God with the righteousness of Christ as a new creature. He has a firm happiness and assurance of salvation and forgiveness of sin.

The stone was shining with a luster of fire. The believer must live with a fire in his soul to win the lost as well as be submissive to the will of God. The splendor of knowing Christ results in true happiness, which God alone can give.

---

[59]Charles W. Slemming, These are the Garments (Chicago, Illinois: Moody Press, 1955) p. 122

Asher would yield to royal dainties, presenting a picture of the believer feasting upon the Word of God. Christians should never stay on milk, but develop an appetite for the meat of the Word. This will enable the believer to grow and mature in his spiritual walk with the Lord.[60]

The iron and brass shoes of Asher represented a strong fortification, a trampling underfoot of evil. The strong Christian enjoys a fruitful and overcoming life.

The strength of Asher would number the days of his life. The believer is possessed with strength beyond his finite powers and abilities. He is possessed with the power and strength of the indwelling Holy Spirit, which enables him to live a successful and victorious Christian life.

Jasper

The name of Naphtali was engraved on the jasper. The stone may be found in many colors, but the most common is yellow. Others are found in scarlet, red, crimson, green, various browns, and one is green with red spots known as the bloodstone. Many of the stones are transparent and others opaque. The color of the stone on the Breastplate was probably transparent. Christ, sitting on the throne in the Book of Revelation, was like jasper and a sardius stone. The walls of the Holy City were made of jasper.[61]

Naphtali was born of Bilhah and adopted by Rachel. Rachel said, "With great wrestling have I wrestled with my sister, and I have prevailed: and she called his name Naphtali." (Genesis 30:7-8) "In bestowing this name she had a reference, in the opinion of some, to her bitter

---

[60]Charles W. Slemming, These are the Garments (Chicago, Illinois: Moody Press, 1955) p. 129
[61]Charles W. Slemming, These are the Garments (Chicago, Illinois: Moody Press, 1955) p. 140

contentions and rivalry with her sister, but in the judgment of others, to her wrestling with God in prayer."[62]

"The evil lies in the system, which being a violation of God's original ordinance, cannot yield happiness."[63]

Man has wrestled with God from since the beginning of his creation. Man wrestles his habits, his conscience and his temptations. The Holy Spirit convicts and deals with the conscience of man and he is in a continuous wrestling match until he surrenders totally to the Lord.

One must remember the wrestlings Christ endured while upon the earth. He wrestled in prayer at Gethsemane, wrestled the temptations of the devil in the wilderness and wrestled with death on Calvary, but He was the victor of every match He faced.

"The result of Christ's wrestling means the birth of many spiritual Naphtalis-believers, and we too must know something of wrestling in our spiritual life for we are called to warfare."[64] "For we wrestle not against flesh and blood, but against principalities, against powers, against the rulers of darkness of this world, against spiritual wickedness in high places." (Ephesians 6:12) The believer must put on the whole armour of God and be prepared as a soldier for war to battle off the enemy of the world, the flesh and the devil. The Christian's life is one continuous battlefield. The old nature struggles against the new nature. The old man would delight in defeating the new man, but through Christ one may have a total victory no matter what the peril may be.

---

[62] Robert Jamieson, A.R. Fausset, & David Brown, Critical and Experimental Commentary, Vol. 1 (Grand Rapids, Michigan: W. B. Eerdmans Publishing Company, 1945) p. 204
[63] Robert Jamieson, A.R. Fausset & David Brown, Commentary on the Whole Bible (Grand Rapids, Michigan: Zondervan Publishing House, 1974) p. 35
[64] Charles W. Slemming, These are the Garments (Chicago, Illinois: Moody Press, 1955) p. 136.

The Memorial

"And thou shalt put the two stones upon the shoulders of the ephod, for stones of memorial unto the children of Israel: and Aaron shall bear their names before the Lord upon his two shoulders for a memorial." (Exodus 28:12)

"And he put them (the onyx-stones) on the shoulders of the ephod, that they should be stones for a memorial to the children of Israel, as the Lord commanded." (Exodus 39:7)

"And Aaron shall bear the names of the children of Israel in the breastplate of judgment upon his heart, when he goeth in unto the holy place, for a memorial before the Lord continually." (Exodus 28:29)

The memorial served a two-fold purpose. First, it reminded the children of Israel of their deliverance from bondage in Egypt by the blood of the paschal lamb. Secondly, the precious stones gave a constant assurance that the children of Israel had been accepted by God, because their names were engraved on the stones which rested on the shoulders of the high priest.
The believer has two memorials, which should be kept in remembrance of his redemption through the precious blood of Jesus Christ, our Saviour. The blood of Christ is a constant reminder that the believer has been delivered from the bondage of sin and the penalty of sin. The believer stands before God as His children upheld in His presence, by the beauty and glory of His Son.[65]

---

[65] Henry W. Soltau, The Tabernacle (Fincastle, Virginia: Scripture Truth Book Company) p. 249

The names of the children of Israel were worn on the shoulders of the high priest as a memorial before the Lord. When Aaron entered the holy place, it reminded God of the love and perfection in which Israel stood accepted before Him. The candlestick, with its sevenfold light and the glory of God from the Cherubim, sent forth a brilliancy that so attracted the eyes of the Lord. In like manner, the believer has Christ, the Great High Priest, as a memorial before the Lord to present them spotless with His love, power and bright glory.

<u>Continually</u>. "Thou shalt set upon the table shewbread before me always, or continually." Exodus 24:8)

>   A. With the candlestick; "to cause the lamp to burn always, or continually." (Exodus 27:20)
>
>   B. With the incense; "a perpetual, or continual incense before the Lord." (Exodus 30:8)
>
>   C. With the burnt offering and the fire on the altar. (Exodus 29: 38, 42)
>
>   D. With the meat offering. (Leviticus 6:20)
>
>   E. With the golden plate on the forehead of the High Priest. (Exodus 28:38)

These tell us of the continuous presence of Christ before God on our behalf. He lives forever to make intercession for the believers. Every person in Christ is complete and accepted in the beloved. His mediation on our behalf has never failed, although our faith may have been weak at times.[66]

---

[66]Henry W. Soltau, <u>The Tabernacle</u> (Fincastle, Virginia: Scripture Truth Book Company). p. 250.

The reason the believer can continue to fight and stand through the storms of life is because he has one in glory that assures him of constant intercession and power. Because Christ lives, the believer can face tomorrow with a smile on his face and a joy in his heart.

The Urim and the Thummim

"And thou shalt put in the breastplate of judgment the Urim and the Thummim: and they shall be upon Aaron's heart when he goeth in before the Lord: and Aaron shall bear the judgment of the children of Israel upon his heart continually." (Exodus 28:30)

The breastplate was folded to form a bag into which the Urim and the Thummin were put. As to what the Urim and Thummim were no one has decided at the present. Urim means "lights" while Thummim means "perfections." The Septuagint translates the two words as "Manifestation and Truth."[67] All of the meanings direct thoughts to the Lord Jesus Christ. He was the light of the world. In Him was light. He was the perfect Son of God. He was tempted in every way man has been tempted and yet without sin. He was the manifestation of the likeness of God. He is the expressed image of the invisible God. Jesus came to reveal God to the human race. He was manifested in the flesh and pointed out the nature of God. Last, He is the truth. He presents the ultimate truth of God and His Word through His Deity and His humanity.

Urim is also translated "fire" and "fires."[68] The vision of Christ in the Book of Revelation in the midst of the seven

---

[67]Henry W. Soltau, The Tabernacle (Fincastle, Virginia: Scripture Truth Book Company) p. 251
[68]Ibid., P. 253

golden candlesticks, describes His eyes as a flame of fire. The eyes of the Lord never slumber nor sleep. He has a constant watch over the world as it travails in the wickedness produced by man. Man may seek to hide from the presence and eyes of the Lord, but his efforts are futile.

Actually no man has been able to find out what the Urim and Thummim were. They may have been used in deciding the Divine will of God in critical matters. It is a great possibility that they could have been black and white stones – the black representing negative; the white representing positive. The believer has an Urim and a Thummim---the Old and New Testaments. These are the believer's light to the critical situation they face. Searching the Word for the will of God can solve every situation.

"The whole life course is mapped out in the New and Old Testament. The Testaments are never to be separated: they are to be read together, they explain one another; torn asunder, they lose their unity and their music; brought together, you bring flower to root, you bring the noonday to dawn, you unite things, forces and ministries never to be dissevered."[69]

The Mitre

"And thou shalt make the mitre of fine linen." (Exodus 28:39)

"And a mitre of fine linen." (Exodus 39:28)

"The Hebrew word Mitznepheth, here translated Mitre, and is used exclusively for the head-dress of the high priest, except in one passage."

---

[69]Charles W. Slemming, These are the Garments (Chicago, Illinois: Moody Press, 1955) p. 153

(Ezekiel 11:26)[70] It is derived from a very signifying "to roll, or wind round;" possibly intimating that the high priest's mitre was wound around his head, like a tiara.

"There is another word kindred to this, Tzaneeph, translated Diadem."[71] The word probably means a band. This was an emblem of royalty in the East.

The first purpose of the mitre seems to be for the covering of the head. Many times in the Bible the covering of the head was a token of self-humiliation, grief and shame. In modern days a covering is worn as a sign of mourning.

Paul directed the woman to cover her head because the man is the head of woman. The man's head is to be uncovered because he is the image and the glory of God. "In the assemblies therefore of the people of God, the woman, standing as a representative of the Church is subjection to Christ, covers her head; the man, being a type of Christ Himself as the Head of the Church, Un-covers his head."[72]

This may indicate that the mitre covered the head of the high priest in order to present a picture of being subject to God and that he was standing in His presence. Even thought the high priest officiated as the people's spokesman, he too must stand in humility before God because of his sin.

The mitre also stood for holiness or righteousness. It was a covering of responsibility and leadership. This presents a picture of the holiness and righteousness of Christ.

The head controls the whole body. It denotes authority. Christ is the Head of the Church and controls it. The head also denotes wisdom. Old age and white hair tell

---

[70]Henry W. Soltau, The Tabernacle (Fincastle, Virginia: Scripture Truth Book Company) p. 266

[71]Charles W. Slemming, These are the Garments (Chicago, Illinois: Moody Press, 1955) p. 266

[72]Charles W. Slemming, These are the Garments (Chicago, Illinois: Moody Press, 1955) p. 267

of the experienced life, which can impart much wisdom. The Book of Revelation tells of Christ in the midst of the seven candlesticks and "His head and His hairs were white like wool, white as snow...." (Rev. 1:14) Instead of coming as the savior, Christ now comes as the judge, denoted by the white hair.

"Our High Priest, the Son of God, has the wisdom of God in eternity. He has manifested the wisdom of God, and the power of God, in redemption. And he exercises in perfect righteousness, and in entire subjection, all this wisdom and power on behalf of the saints of the Most High."[73]

The Golden Plate

> "And thou shalt make a plate of pure gold, and engrave upon it, like the engraving of a signet, HOLINESS TO THE LORD.
> "And thou shalt put it on a blue lace, that it may be upon the mitre; upon the forefront of the mitre it shall be.
> "And it shall be upon Aaron's forehead, that Aaron may bear the iniquity of the holy things which the children of Israel shall hallow in all their holy gifts; and it shall be always upon his forehead, that they may be accepted before the Lord." (Exodus 28:36-38)

> "And they made the plate of the holy crown of pure gold, and wrote upon it a writing, like to the engraving of a signet, HOLINESS TO THE LORD.

---

[73] Henry W. Soltau, The Tabernacle (Fincastle, Virginia: Scripture Truth Book Company) p. 268

"And they tied unto it a lace of blue, to fasten it on high upon the mitre; as the Lord commanded Moses." (Exodus 39:30,31)

The object of the mitre was to enable the high priest to wear the golden plate before the Lord.

"The Hebrew word here translated "plate" is "tsits" and elsewhere is translated "flower" and "blossom," as in the flowers which adorned the pillars of Solomon's Temple – Jachin and Boaz."[74] The holy crown adds beauty, charm and grace to the brow of the High Priest. The holiness of God hallows the head of the believer. "As for man, his days are as the grass: as the flower of the field, so he flourisheth." (Psalms 53:15)

Man, with all of his boasting, self-glorification and manhood, is nothing more than the fading grass, or the flower that fades. His life exists one minute and then fades away. "Against all this brevity, uncertainty, and fading, there stands in contrast that lasting beauty, that glorious certainty, that permanent quality that belongeth to the man whose life is crowned with the fragrant blossom of holiness."[75]

Notice the position of the golden plate. It was upon the forehead of Aaron. The forehead is a symbol of will and intellect. It was said of rebellious Israel, "...for all the house of Israel are stiff of forehead, and hard of heart." (Ezekiel 3:7) This verse and others describe the will and the character of the rebellious man's mind.

The Bible teaches that the worst form of leprosy was found on the forehead. He was pronounced totally unclean by the priest and had to put his hand over his mouth and cry: "Unclean, unclean!" The story of King Uzziah, who entered the Temple of the Lord to burn incense to the Lord, is

---

[74]Charles W. Slemming, <u>These are the Garments</u> (Chicago, Illinois: Moody Press, 1955) p. 160

[75]Ibid. p. 161

recorded in the Book of II Chronicles. Because of desecrating the Temple, God judged him with leprosy on his forehead. This gives a vivid picture of the rebellion of the natural unsaved man.

The HOLINESS TO THE LORD must be written not only on our foreheads but every facet of our life. The believer's mind, body, soul, spirit, tongue, lips, hands, feet and every member must be yielded to the holiness of God. The reader notices also that the inscription was only given to the high priest, and not to the others. The Lord said, "Be ye holy even as I am Holy."

"HOLINESS TO THE LORD must be so written upon the forehead of the believer that all who converse with them may see, and say, that they bear the
image of God's holiness, and are devoted to the praise of it."[76]

The golden plate was secured by a ribbon of blue, typifying both Grace and Divinity. Aaron could only bear the iniquity of the holy things as the grace of God was given to him.

The Embroidered Coat

"And thou shalt embroider the coat of fine linen." (Exodus 38:39)

"And they made coats of fine linen." (Exodus 39:27)

The coat from a distance would appear ordinary, but a closer examination would reveal that it was made with much skill and beauty. "The root word used of "embroider" gives us the same idea as our modern "damask," an embroidery not worked on but skillfully worked into the material."[77]

---

[76] Matthew Henry, Matthew Henry's Commentary, Vol. 1 (Westwood, New Jersey: Fleming H. Revell Company). p. 443.

[77] Charles W. Slemming, These are the Garments (Chicago, Illinois: Moody Press, 1955) p. 30

At a shallow glance one would see Christ as an ordinary man, but closer examination of His life and works will reveal the beauty of splendor of His name and Person.

The coat was made of fine linen, which cannot be purchased today. It was an Egyptian art that ceased when they died. The Egyptians manufactured linen and other clothes that were of superior quality. The produce of their looms was exported to foreign nations. The embroidered work of the Egyptians was highly esteemed. The quality of one piece of the linen was comparable to that of silk, and not inferior in texture to our finest cambric. One must notice then how God brought the Israelites through the wilderness to possess these materials to be used as a part of the priestly garments.

The Hebrew word "Kethoneth" here is translated "Coat."[78] "And Jehovah God doth make to the man, and to his wife coats (Kethoneths) of skin and doth clothe them." (Genesis 3:21) Notice that the coats were made of skin. This indicates that the one sacrifice was sufficient for both. When Adam and Eve sinned against God in the Garden of Eden, they sowed fig leaves together and tried to hide their nakedness. God's penetrating eyes saw through the fig leaves of self-righteousness and came to clothe them in the skins of an innocent animal. These coverings hid their shame and their ungodliness. The blood of this innocent, faultless animal had to be shed in order to cover their naked shame. The coat of fine linen may have represented the Righteous Servant. "By His knowledge shall my righteous servant justify many, for He shall bear their iniquities" (Isaiah 30:2).

The High Priest and the Priest wore the garment, but the garment was the high Priest's undergarment while it was the priest's only garment. This pictures the believer having the imputed righteousness of Christ in their lives. The

---

[78]Charles W. Slemming, These are the Garments (Chicago, Illinois: Moody Press, 1955) p. 31

believer has been clothed with the righteousness of the Righteous Servant. "I will greatly rejoice in the Lord, my soul shall be joyful in my God; for He hath clothed me with the garments of salvation, He hath covered me with the robe of righteousness...."(Isaiah 56:10)

The coat was put on the Priest the moment he washed. This was untrue of Christ. He was clothed with the garments of glory from the beginning. When He took off the coat of glory to come to this sin cursed earth, He remained spotless and sinless and there was no need of washing.[79]

The Girdle of the Priest

"A broidered coat, a mitre, and a girdle. And thou shalt make the girdle of needlework." (Exodus 28:4, 39)

"And a girdle of fine twined linen, and blue, and purple, and scarlet needlework." (Exodus 39:29)

It has already been stated the "curious girdle" was not a true girdle in the sense of the word. The true girdle of the Priest is described in these few verses. "The Hebrew word is exclusively used for this inner girdle, and that of the High Priest on the Day of Atonement, and for the girdles of the Priests; except in one other instance, (Isaiah 26:21), where Eliakim is to be clothed with Shebna's robe, (coat) and strengthened with his girdle."[80]

"This girdle was made of the same materials as those of the Vail; but the order of their arrangement was that of the

---

[79] Henry W. Soltau, The Tabernacle (Fincastle, Virginia: Scripture Truth Book Company) p. 286
[80] Ibid., p. 289.

innermost curtains of the Tabernacle, fine linen, blue, purple, scarlet."[81]

The fine linen, which comes first, is a type of righteousness. Righteous- ness shall be the girdle of his loins, and faithfulness, the girdle of his reins." (Isaiah 6:5) The righteousness and faithfulness of Christ ultimated at the cross, proving both. Faithfulness seems to be the same as truth.

The girdle strengthened the loins for service. Beneath the garments, the High Priest was preserved as the girded righteous servant of the Lord. This typifies Christ with all His majestic power and glory, and yet He delights to remain the Righteous Servant of the Father.

The girdle is also a symbol of service. The girded loins denote the readiness for action. This was true of the priest as is certainly true of Christ, the Great High Priest. He lives forever to make intercession for the believers.[82]

The girdle was attached to the undergarments and was not seen except on the Day of Atonement. The believer many times is not conscious of Christ's interceding power because there is no outward evidence that he may see. The believer knows Christ promised to intercede, but he cannot see Him with His physical eyes. The evidence of His intercession is completed when the believer sees his prayers answered.

"The fine linen coat, and the girdle of needlework, was as much garments for glory and beauty, as the gorgeous ephod with its breastplate of precious stones."[83]

"The glory and beauty of spotless righteousness and obedience, manifested to the full here below in every scene

---

[81] Henry W. Soltau. The Tabernacle (Fincastle, Virginia: Scripture Truth Book Company) p. 289

[82] Charles W. Slemming, These are the Garments (Chicago, Illinois: Moody Press, 1955) p. 34

[83] Henry W. Soltau, The Tabernacle (Fincastle, Virginia: Scripture Truth Book Company) p. 294

and circumstance of human life: perfected in the suffering of the cross in death, and now perpetuated for ever in the holiest above."[84]

---

[84]Ibid., P. 294

Chapter 4

THE GARMENTS FOR AARON'S SONS

"And for Aaron's sons thou shalt make coats. And thou shalt make for them girdles, and bonnets shalt thou make for them for glory and for beauty." (Exodus 28:40)

"And they made coats of fine linen of woven work for Aaron and for his sons.
"And goodly bonnets of fine linen." (Exodus 39: 27, 28)

The garments worn by Aaron's sons consisted of coats, girdles, and bonnets of fine twined linen. They had no gold, brilliant colors, ornaments, or embroidery. They were clothed with pure white garments.
The sons of Aaron stood in no official dignity, but did have access to the holy place in which they ministered at the altar. They did not represent people on their behalf, but rather instructed the people on the holy things of God. They were types of the heavenly priesthood. The twenty-four elders in the Book of Revelation entailed a priestly standing, which formed the heavenly council. They were not only elders, but judges as well. "They are clothed in white raiment, as priests, and they have on their heads crowns of gold, that is, victor's crowns, or chaplets."[85]
The multitude is seen clothed with white robes and a priestly company serves night and day in the heavenly temple of God. The bride of Christ is seen clothed in fine clean linen and white. This represents the righteousness of the saints. The white raiment is also alluded to in Revelation

---

[85]Henry W. Soltau, The Tabernacle (Fincastle, Virginia: Scripture Truth Book Company) p. 295

chapter three. Thus the believer stands before God, spotless and righteous, not his righteousness, but the righteousness of God imputed to him by faith.

Christ is the believer's robe of righteousness. Paul exhorted the believers also to put on the Lord Jesus, admonishing them to walk correspondingly to their real standing with God. The believer's thoughts, walk, and conduct should be those of Christ Himself. The believers have the mind of Christ and should let the Holy Spirit utilize that mind in conducting their lives.

The Girdles

Moses was directed by the Lord to grid Aaron and his sons with girdles.

The New Testament alludes to the girdle as a part of the believer's armour.

"Wherefore take unto you the whole armour of God, that ye may be able to stand in the evil day, having done all to stand.
"Stand therefore having your loins girt about with truth, and having on the breastplate of righteousness:
"And your feet shod with the preparation of the gospel of peace;
"Above all taking the shield of faith, wherewith ye shall be able to quench all the fiery darts of the wicked.
"And take the helmet of salvation, and the sword of the spirit, which is the word of God." (Ephesians 6:13-17)

The beginning of the Epistle tells us that the believer is seated with Christ in heavenly places and then that the believer is to stand. This gives the assurance of the inheritance that the believers have in Christ. The believer has been accepted in the beloved and made heirs with God and joint-heirs with Christ.

The girdle is first mentioned in these verses. The sword is mentioned last. The entire strength of the warrior's ability to stand rests upon the firmness of the girdle. Satan will utterly cast him down if his loins are weak. The Word of God is the believer's support and weapon, represented by the girdle and the sword.

"The Girdle is also an important part of the ordinary garments of the believer, as a priest and servant."[86]

The Lord admonished His disciples, "Let your loins be girded about, and your lights burning; and ye yourselves like unto men that wait for their Lord." (Luke 12: 35.36)

The believer will not be in a state of expectancy if he does not let the truth and light of the gospel dominate his life. The inactive believer becomes worldly-minded, and indulges in the things of the world.

Peter gives this exhortation to the believers: "Wherefore gird up the loins of your mind, be sober, and hope to the end for the grace which is to be brought unto you at the revelation of Jesus Christ." (I Peter 1:13). Believers are strangers and pilgrims in this present world. They are foreigners to this world and are looking for that land that is of God.

The verses just read bears a great application to the Christian's life. The believer who allows his garments to become loose, and does not gird up his loins will make very little progress on the pilgrim journey.[87] The mind of the believer should not be loose with evil imagination, but learn to fix his mind upon the things pertaining to the purity and holiness of God. The pilgrim will also walk unbalanced if he

---

[86]Henry W. Soltau, <u>The Tabernacle</u> (Fincastle, Virginia: Scripture Truth Book Company) p. 299
[87] Ibid. p. 301.

indulges himself in intoxicating draughts.[88] People of the world are filling their minds, hearts and lives and are drowning out the conscious of their soul. The god of the world, Satan, has blinded their minds to the truth of the gospel of Christ. The girded servant of the Lord is to be sober, keeping his mind consecrated to the will of God.

Christ was seen in the Book of Revelation and was, "girt about the paps with a golden girdle."

"The object of this girdle seems not to have been to strengthen Him who wore it for priestly service of judgment, but rather to bind the robe of blue – the robe of the heavenly love and peace firmly around the heart, so that in the midst of searching words of reproof and warning, mercies might be poured forth from the breasts of consolations."[89]

The Bonnets

"And bonnets shalt thou make for them, for glory and for beauty."
(Exodus 28:40)

"And goodly bonnets of fine linen." (Exodus 39:28)
"The word (migbahgohth) translated 'bonnets' only occurs four times, and is exclusively used for the head dress of the Priests. It is derived from a very signifying 'elevation,' often used for a hill."[90] These bonnets bound round the head of the Priest. The bonnets probably consisted of fine linen, which folded like a turban and fitted around the head. "The word translated 'goodly' is worthy of notice. It is rendered 'bonnets,' 'tire of the head,' 'beauty,' and

---

[88] Henry W. Soltau, The Tabernacle (Fincastle, Virginia: Scripture Truth Book Company) p. 301
[89] Henry W. Soltau, The Tabernacle (Fincastle, Virginia: Scripture Truth Book Company) p. 302
[90] Ibid., P. 302

'ornaments' and is derived from a verb, signifying 'to beautify, or glorify.'"[91] This bonnet was definitely used for exaltation, ornament and for glory and beauty.

The thesis has already proven that covering was used to symbolize subjection. The Jew of today covers his head in the synagogue and when he reads his Bible in private. This reveals the constant abiding of the presence of God. Christ has been exalted at the right hand of the Father and now the believer walks in the elevation of submission to the will of God.

The head-tires of white are said to be very ornamental. They were not used for the purpose of attraction, but for adorning. The head-tires were a type of the meek and the quiet spirit in the sight of God. This is of a great price to the Lord. This pictures the dedicated women of old that fully and completely trusted in God, and adorned themselves into subjection of their own husbands.[92]

"There is a 'glory and beauty' in spotless righteousness which may be little accounted of by men, but which enables the believer to approach God with confidence, and fits us for His Holy presence."[93]

The Linen Breeches

"And thou shalt make them linen breeches to cover their nakedness, from the loins even unto the thighs they shall reach;

"And they shalt be upon Aaron, and upon his sons, when they come in unto the tabernacle of the congregation, or when they come near unto the altar

---

[91] Henry W. Soltau, The Tabernacle (Fincastle, Virginia: Scripture Truth Book Company) p. 302
[92] Henry W. Soltau, The Tabernacle (Fincastle, Virginia: Scripture Truth Book Company) p. 303
[93] Ibid., p. 304

to minister in the holy place: That they bear not iniquity, and die: it shall be a statute for ever unto him and his seed after him." (Exodus 28:42,43)

There are great difficulties that arise from the linen breeches. In the Book of Exodus the Hebrew word "bad" and "shehshmash" both occur. This indicates that the two sorts of linen were woven together.[94]

In certain services Aaron and his sons had to put on the linen breeches. "When they came in unto the tabernacle of the congregation, or when they came near unto the altar to minister in the holy place." (Leviticus 8:43) This means that when they came into the holy place to minister or to burn incense at the altar, they had to wear breeches.

The first reaction to sin by man was to cover his own nakedness. Shame and guilt gripped the heart of man as his sins runned rampant. The linen breeches first hide the nakedness of man. This contains a beautiful picture of Christ and his imputed righteousness. The lost, natural man has no righteousness of his own, but truly needs righteousness to enter heaven. The righteousness Christ imputes into the life of the believer becomes a covering for man's nakedness.

Notice that the loins were to reach to the thighs. The entire nature of the natural man is thus concealed and hidden in the nature of God. Christ provided the covering so that they would not have to bear their sins and die. "God's righteous servant justifies many through faith in Him, by having borne their iniquities."[95]

The altar presented a picture of lowliness and self-abasement. The altar was an altar of the earth, standing in contrast with the high places, selected by the self-righteous

---

[94] Henry W. Soltau, The Tabernacle (Fincastle, Virginia: Scripture Truth Book Company) p. 304.

[95] Henry W, Soltau, The Tabernacle (Fincastle, Virginia: Scripture Truth Book Company) p. 306

man. The Bible tells the Christian that they should present their bodies as a living sacrifice. The altar represented the believer as laying his life on the altar of God ready to be used for a sacrifice or service.

      The statute presented the lost man drawing nigh to God and having the guilt and shame of his sin buried out of the sight of God. Not only is the penalty of sin forgiven, but also the guilt of sin. This enables the believer to walk in a perfect peace with God. He has laid down all arms of rebellion and has surrendered totally to the Lordship of Christ.

Chapter 5

THE BEARING UP OF THE TABERNACLE

Because of the importance of the erection of the tabernacle, one will see the necessity of recording these lengthy passages.

"And the Lord spake unto Moses, saying,

"On the first day of the first month shalt thou set up the tabernacle of the tent of the congregation.

"And thou shalt put therein the ark of the testimony, and cover the ark with the vail.

"And thou shalt bring in the table, and set in order the things that are to be set in order upon it; and thou shalt bring in the candlestick, and light the lamps thereof.

"And thou shalt set the altar of gold for the incense before the ark of the testimony, and put the hanging of the door to the tabernacle.

"And thou shalt set the altar of the burnt offering before the door of the tabernacle of the tent of the congregation.

"And thou shalt set the laver between the tent of the congregation and the altar, and shall put water therein.

"And thou shalt set up the court round about, and hang up the hanging at the court gate.

"And thou shalt take the anointing oil, and anoint the tabernacle, and all that is therein, and shalt hallow it and all the vessels thereof: and it shall be holy.

"And thou shalt anoint the altar of the burnt offering, and all his vessels, and sanctify the altar: and it shall be an altar most holy.

"And thou shalt anoint the laver and his foot, and sanctify it.
"And thou shalt bring Aaron and his sons unto the door of the tabernacle of the congregation, and wash them with water." (Exodus 40:1-12)

"And it came to pass in the first month in the second year, on the first day of the month, that the tabernacle was reared up,
"And Moses reared up the tabernacle, and fastened his sockets, and set up the boards thereof, and reared up his pillars.
"And he spread abroad the tent over the tabernacle, and put the covering of the tent above it; as the Lord commanded Moses.
"And he took and put the testimony into the ark, and set the staves on the ark, and put the mercy seat above upon the ark:
"And he brought the ark into the tabernacle, and set up the vail of the covering, and covered the ark of the testimony; as the Lord commanded Moses.
"And he put the table in the tent of the congregation, upon the side of the tabernacle northward, without the vail.
"And he set the bread in order upon it before the Lord; as the Lord commanded Moses.
"And he put the table candlestick in the tent of the congregation, over against the table, on the side of the tabernacle southward.
"And he lighted the lamps before the Lord; as the Lord commanded Moses.
"And he put the golden altar in the tent of the congregation before the vail:
"And he burnt sweet incense thereon; as the Lord commanded Moses.

"And he set up the hanging at the door of the tabernacle.

"And he put the altar of burnt offering by the door of the tabernacle of the tent of the congregation, and offered upon it the burnt offering and the meat offering; as the Lord commanded Moses.

"And he set the laver between the tent of the congregation and the altar, and put water there, to wash withal.

"And Moses and Aaron and his sons washed their hands and their feet thereat:

"When they went into the tent of the congregation, and when they came near unto the altar, they washed; as the Lord commanded Moses.

"And he reared up the court round about the tabernacle and the altar, and set up the hanging of the court gate. So Moses finished the work." (Exodus 40:17-33)

The word "Tabernacle" means dwelling place. It was the dwelling place of God and the center for Israel's worship. The Tabernacle was approximately 75' X 150', and was completely portable. It was built of gold, silver, brass, shittim wood, linen, goats' hair and skins.[96]

The story of the erection of the Tabernacle relates not only a spiritual significance, but also a scientific magnificence. The building was perfect in every detail. "Once completed, it never again required attention, addition, or alteration."[97] The structure was built so well that it lasted approximately five hundred years; forty of those years were in the howling wilderness. The durability of the structure is

---

[96]R. H. Mount, The Law Prophesied (Mansfield, Ohio: Mount Publications, 1966) p. 22.
[97]Stephen F. Olford, The Tabernacle: Camping with God (Neptune, New Jersey: Loizeaux Brothers, Inc., 1971) p. 42

accredited to the fact that God was behind its conception, as well as the construction.

God gave the children of Israel a pattern for the erection of the Tabernacle. First, the erection was heavenly. It was heavenly because the presence of God would meet man there. The believer knows that God dwells in heaven. It is His eternal dwelling place. One will find that at this period in history God chose to meet with man in the Tabernacle. The Tabernacle is heavenly, because it seems to be a replica of something in heaven. Secondly, the Tabernacle was orderly. Notice that each physical structure had a specific place and a spiritual significance. God gave detailed instructions as to how to erect, dismantle and the transporting of the Tabernacle. So it is with the Christian life as Paul states about the order of their life; "Let all things be done decently and in order." (I Corinthians 14:40)

The Lord also gave the children of Israel the provision for the Tabernacle's erection. First, the materials were provided for the erection. The children of Israel found favor in the sight of many Egyptians and received jewels of silver and of gold. The foresight of God knew that eventually the materials would be used in the construction of the Tabernacle.

The people were willing to donate the materials sacrificially. "They came, every one whose heart stirred him up, and every one whom his spirit made willing, and they brought the Lord's offering to the work of the Tabernacle of the congregation, and for all his service, and for the holy garments." (Exodus 35:21) The Bible records the incident and points out the fact that Moses had to restrain the people from donating more materials. It has been estimated that their donations amounted to nearly a million dollars in American money.[98] This reminds the believer of the responsibilities of giving sacrificially to the work of the Lord.

---

[98]Stephen F. Olford, The Tabernacle: Camping with God (Neptune, New Jersey: Loizeaux Brothers, Inc., 1971) p. 46

There has never been a Christian in the history of Christianity that has out-given the Lord. May the Lord help believers to see this necessity.

The diversity of the materials was tremendous. The metals consisted of gold, silver and copper. The colors amounted to blue, purple, and scarlet. In fabrics, fine linen, goat's hair, ram's skins and badgers skins were used. The incorruptible acacia wood structured the building with oil used as lighting and anointing.[99] The stones consisted of rare quality, which were used for the High Priest's breastplate. Each person gave to a capacity, which they could afford. Those who had no substance donated their time to the construction of the Tabernacle, thus involving everyone.

As to the manpower of the structure, one will see where God gave special talents to different people. The workmanship was by a divine appointment of God. The Holy Spirit utilized every man and woman until the structure was completed. God works in this manner through Christians today. He appoints or calls them to special ministries and by the leadership of the Holy Spirit accomplishes the work.

God also had a position for the erection of the Tabernacle. In the days of Moses, the Bedouins journeyed from place to place under the supervision of their sheik. The sheik would lead the way with a long spear, resting on the side of the camel.

When he chose a spot to make camp he would put the spear into the ground. This was a sign of a resting place. The servants would then proceed to erect the master's tent behind the spear and pitch their tents in a circle around the tent of the sheik. The sheik dwelt in the midst of his servants. When he chose to move on, he would remove the spear and the rest would follow.[100]

---

[99] Ibid. p. 47
[100] Stephen F. Olford, The Tabernacle: Camping with God (Neptune, New Jersey: Loizeaux Brothers Inc., 1971) p. 49

This becomes a tremendous picture of God (Chieftan) leading the children of Israel through the wilderness all those triffling years. "His spear was the pillar of cloud and of fire."[101] When the cloud moved, they moved until God planted the divine spear.

The reader will then notice the position of the structure in relation to the compass. The Tabernacle always was constructed toward the East, looking at the sunrise each new day. This pictures the attitude of the optimistic Christian, looking forward to each new and bright day to work in the service of the Lord.

Notice also the position of the structure in relation to the camp. The Tabernacle was always to be centrally located. Two-and-half million Jews encompassed the structure in a twelve-mile radius.[102]

"On the East were tents of Isachar 54,400; Judah 74,600; Zebulon 57,400 men; on the West were the tents of Manasseh 32,200; Ephraim 40,500; Benjamin 35,400 men; on the North were the tents of Asher 41,500; Dan 62,700; Naphtali 53,400 men; on the South were the tents of Simeon 59,300; Reuben 46,500; Gad 45, 650 men. Then flanking the Tabernacle on all sides was the tribe of Levi, divided into four families: on the East, Moses, Aaron, and the sons of Aaron the Priests; on the West, the Gershonites 7,500; on the North, the Merarites 6,200; on the South, the Kohathites 8,600[103].

There was enough space between the Tabernacle and the first line of tents, to gather the nation before God for worship and instruction in the Word of God.

The only tribe allowed to pitch their tent near the Tabernacle was the tribe of Levi because they were charged

---

[101] Ibid. p. 50
[102] Stephen F. Olford, The Tabernacle: Camping with God (Neptune, New Jersey: Loizeaux Brothers Inc., 1971) p. 50
[103] Stephen F. Olford, The Tabernacle: Camping with God (Neptune, New Jersey: Loiseaux Brothers Inc., 1971) p. 50

by God to care for the Tabernacle, as well as carry out the ministry of worship. They had a double responsibility of preserving peace among the people, "that there be no wrath upon the congregation," and to "keep the charge of the Tabernacle testimony." (Numbers 1:53)

God also had a period for the erection of the Tabernacle. God did not tell the children of Israel to build the Tabernacle until He brought them out of the bondage of Egypt.[104] The Book of Exodus makes it quite clear that it took Israel two-and-a-half to three months to reach Mount Sinai.[105] The work commenced after Moses came down from the Mount, in which Moses remained for forty days and forty nights. Secondly, the Tabernacle was completed on the first day of the first month, in the second year of Israel's journeying. This definitely means that the Tabernacle was erected and completed on New Year's Day.

Egypt represents the natural man in bondage to sin. The deliverance from Egypt pictures the sinner being delivered from sin. Notice that the Tabernacle was not built until the children of Israel were out of Egypt. The Tabernacle became the dwelling place for the Lord. Until a lost man is delivered from sin, God will not indwell his body. When that man receives Christ as his Lord and Saviour, Christ comes into his life and body as a dwelling place.[106]

---

[104]Charles H. Stevens, The Wilderness Journey (Chicago, Illinois: Moody Press, 1975) p. 22

[105]Joseph Parker, Preaching Through the Bible vol. 1 (Grand Rapids, Michigan: Baker Book House, 1975) p. 148-149

[106] Stephen F. Olford, The Tabernacle: Camping with God (Neptune, New Jersey: Loizeaux Brothers Inc., 1971) p. 52

Chapter 6

THE CONSECRATION OF THE PRIEST

"And this is the thing that thou shalt do unto them to hallow them, to minister unto me in the priest's office: Take one young bullock, and two rams without blemish,
"And unleavened bread, and cakes unleavened tempered with oil, and wafers unleavened anointed with oil: of wheaten flour shalt thou make them.
"And thou shalt put them into one basket, and bring them in the basket, with the bullock and the two rams.
"And Aaron and his sons thou shalt bring unto the door of the tabernacle of the congregation, and shalt wash them with water.
"And thou shalt take the garments, and put upon Aaron the coat, and the robe of the ephod, and the ephod, and the breastplate, and gird him with the curious girdle of the ephod:
"And thou shalt put the mitre upon his head, and put the holy crown upon the mitre." (Exodus 29:1-6)

"And the Lord spake unto Moses, saying,
"Take Aaron and his sons with him, and the garments, and the anointing oil, and a bullock for the sin offering, and two rams, and a basket of unleavened bread;
"And gather thou all the congregation together unto the door of the Tabernacle of the congregation.
"And Moses did as the Lord commanded him; and the assembly was gathered together unto the door of the tabernacle of the congregation.
"And Moses said unto the congregation, this is the thing which the Lord commanded to be done.

"And Moses brought Aaron and his sons, and washed them with water."

"And he put upon him the coat, and girded him with the girdle, and clothed him with the robe, and put the ephod upon him, and he girded him with the curious girdle of the ephod, and bound it unto him therewith.

"And he put the breastplate upon him: also he put in the breastplate the Urim and the Thummim.

"And he put the mitre upon his head; also upon the mitre even upon his forefront, did he put the golden plate, the holy crown; as the Lord commanded Moses." (Leviticus 8:1-9)

Aaron and his sons were taken from among the children of Israel. Christ was called out by God to be the Great High Priest. He did not call himself out of a self-will attitude, but rather was chosen by His Father. Notice also the children of God are called out and are a part of His priestly house. He has called the believer out of the darkness into the glorious light of the gospel of Christ.

Secondly, the sons of Aaron and himself were brought to the door of the Tabernacle. The ceremony was then conducted in the presence of the Lord and the presence of the people. This brought them near to God that they might be a blessing to the people. Christ was brought from the dead and is now in the presence of God as the Great High Priest for the children of God, to make intercession for them. God in Christ has brought the believer out of spiritual deadness into the family and presence of God through the mediation of Jesus Christ.

"This was the only time when Aaron and his sons were washed by another with water."[107] They had been instructed to wash their feet and hands on other occasions, but now their entire body was to be washed.

---

[107] Henry W. Soltau, The Tabernacle (Fincastle, Virginia: Scripture Truth Book Company) p. 340

The washing of the priest symbolized the complete cleansing. This refers to the washing of regeneration in the New Testament. "The precious blood of Christ, the true Laver of regeneration, not only cleanses, so as to free us from wrath and judgment, but makes us altogether personally clean, in order that we may with confidence draw near to God."[108]

One will also notice that Aaron was clothed separately from his sons. First, Aaron put on the coat. This is the embroidered coat the study mentioned earlier. Second, he girded himself with the girdle of needlework. These were the innermost garments. Third, he put on the robe and the ephod and girded himself with the curious girdle. Fourth, he put on the breastplate with the Urim and the Thummim inside. Last, he placed the mitre upon his head along with the holy crown. Aaron was then completely clothed with the garments for glory and beauty.[109] The display of Aaron's clothing, commits the reader to the remembrance of the prodigal son. When he came home from the far country of sin, the Father put his best robe on his son. When the lost man receives Christ as his Lord and Saviour, the Father puts a robe of righteousness on him. He is made righteous in the sight of God, fit for heaven, and the presence of God. The garments also typify the glory and beauty of Christ. Christ has been given a name that is above every name, and it will ring throughout eternity.

The Priests were also anointed with oil. This oil is displayed in the Word of God very vividly:

"Moreover the Lord spake unto Moses, saying,

"Take thou also unto thee principal spices, of pure myrrh five hundred shekels, and of sweet cinnamon half so much, even two hundred and fifty shekels, and of sweet calamus two hundred and fifty shekels,

---

[108] Ibid. p. 343
[109] Henry W. Soltau, The Tabernacle (Fincastle, Virginia: Scripture Truth Book Company) p. 344

"And of cassia five hundred shekels, after the shekel of the sanctuary, and of olive oil and hin:
'And thou shalt make it an oil of holy ointment, an ointment compound after the art of the apothecary: it shall be holy anointing oil.
'And thou shalt anoint the tabernacle of the congregation therewith, and the ark of the testimony,
'And the table and all his vessels, and the candlestick and his vessels, and the altar of incense,
"And the altar of burnt offering with all his vessels, and the laver and his foot.
"And thou shalt sanctify them, that they may be most holy: whatsoever toucheth them shall be holy.
"And thou shalt anoint Aaron and his sons, and consecrate them that they may minister unto me in the priest's office.
"And thou shalt speak unto the children of Israel, saying, this shall be an holy anointing oil unto me throughout your generations.
"Upon man's flesh shall it not be poured, neither shall ye make any other like it, after the composition of it: It is holy, and it shall be holy unto you.
"Whosoever compoundeth any like it, or whosoever putteth any of it upon a stranger, shall be cut off from his people." (Exodus 30: 22-33)

The oil was mingled with four spices: Myrrh, cinnamon, calamus, and cassia.

Myrrh is always translated "liberty" in the Hebrew.[110] This symbolizes the mission of Christ because He came to proclaim liberty to the captives. Christ gives liberty to the believer because he has been set free from the captivity of the devil.

---

[110] Henry w. Soltau, The Tabernacle (Fincastle, Virginia: Scripture Truth Book Company) p. 345

The cinnamon and the calamus are plants of the enclosed garden and are used as perfume for the bed. The calamus can be translated as a "measuring rod."

The cassia only occurs two times in the Bible. It has been suggested that it springs from a root which signifies "to cleave" and also "to stoop' and "bow down."[111]

The sons of Aaron were anointed with the oil, but Aaron was the only one, which the oil was poured upon. He was the anointed one of the house. This pictures Christ as the Anointed of God. The word "Christ" itself means, "Anointed One." Christ was the Anointed One of God to carry out the mission of redemption for mankind. "The anointing oil is also a type of the Pentecostal Spirit, and everything connected with the service and worship of God should be in the unction and power of the Holy Spirit of the ascended Christ."[112]

Aaron and his sons then laid their hands upon the head of the ram. This is called "the ram of consecration or fillings." "Not only is the priesthood founded upon sacrifice, but with the preciousness of that sacrifice the hands of the priest are filled."[113] This pictures Christ within the heavenly veil, bringing to God the remembrance of the offering that His people on earth plead. The Bible states, "If we confess our sins, He is faithful and just to forgive us our sins and to cleanse us from all unrighteousness." (I John 1:9)

"He slew it; and Moses took the blood of it, and put it on the tip of Aaron's right ear, and upon the thumb of his right hand, and upon the great toe of his right foot." (Leviticus 8:23)

Aaron was thus sanctified or set apart by the blood of the animal. Christ set Himself apart through His atoning

---

[111] Ibid. p. 347
[112] Thomas Newberry, Types of Levitical Offerings (Bible Study Classics) p. 65
[113] Thomas Newberry, Types of Levitical Offerings (Bible Study Classics) p. 67

death as the Eternal Son of the Living God. The believer also is set apart from the world unto God by the blood of Jesus Christ. The blood of Christ makes the believer clean from sin, plus accepted in the family of God.

Chapter 7

SUMMARY

The study has given hopeful light to the typology of the High Priest. It involved a critical illustrative look at the High Priest in relation to Christ, the Great High Priest. Each garment was described in detail pointing to a biblical truth. Not only did the thesis entail a comparative study on the High Priest, but also the sons of Aaron and their symbolical meaning were discussed. The Tabernacle was observed from a brief orientation. The highlights were discussed bringing the meaning and typology of the High Priest to a conclusive climax.

God has chosen Christ to represent mankind in redemption. The high priest has to make atonement for his sins as well as the people's, but Christ was altogether lovely and perfect and needed no redemption or forgiveness. The high priest offered a sin offering unto the Lord for the forgiveness of their sins and to make propitiation for the people. Christ made atonement or propitiation for the sins of the world and not for Himself.

The Old Testament high priest was to offer daily successions of sacrifices, while the sacrifice Christ made was the all-sufficient sacrifice never needed to be repeated again. His sacrifice has changed the lives of men; women, boys and girls down through the ages while the sacrifices of the high priest did not change the nature or the character of the person. The sacrifices of Christ have made a drastic transformation in the lives of so-called hard cases. People that seemingly have no hope of ever finding peace and joy, have come to experience the life-changing power of the Lord Jesus Christ. Drunkards have been made sober, harlots have been made into respectable and constructive mothers and the drug addict has become a child of God addicted to the power of the Holy Spirit. The life-giving Christ reigns throughout eternity enabling everyone that comes to Him to find contentment, peace, joy, happiness and direction in their lives. "In Him we live and move and have our being." (Acts 17:28)

BIBLIOGRAPHY

Berry, George R. <u>The Interlinear Greek-English New Testament,</u> Grand Rapids, Michigan: Zondervan Publishing House, 1974.

Chamber, Laurence T. <u>Tabernacle Studies Illustrated,</u> Grand Rapids, Michigan: Zondervan Publishing Company

Dehaan, M. R., The <u>Tabernacle</u>, Grand Michigan: Zondervan Publishing House, 1969.

Gaebelein, Arno C, <u>The Annotated Bible</u>, 6 volumes, Neptune, New Jersey: Loizeaux Brothers, Inc. 1970.

Greene, Oliver B. <u>Our Savior</u>, Greenville, South Carolina: Gospel Hours, Inc., 1969.

Greene, Oliver B. <u>The Epistle of Paul the Apostle to the Hebrews</u>, Greenville, South Carolina: The Gospel Hour, Inc., 1969.

Haldeman, I. M. <u>The Tabernacle, Priesthood and Offerings</u>, Westwood, New Jersey: Fleming H. Revell Company.

Henry, Matthew, <u>Matthew Henry's Commentary</u>, 6 volumes, Westwood, New Jersey: Fleming H. Revell Company.

<u>Holy Bible</u>, Authorized King James Version, The Schofield Reference Edition, New York, New York: Oxford University Press, 1945.

<u>Holy Bible</u>, Authorized King James Version, Pilgrim Edition, New York, New York: Fleming University Press, 1952.

Jamieson, Robert, A. R. Fausset and David Brown. Commentary on the Whole Bible, Grand Rapids Michigan: Zondervan Publishing House, 1974.

Jamieson, Robert, A. R. Fausset and David Brown, Critical and Experimental Commentary, 6 volumes, Grand Rapids, Michigan: W. B. Eerdmans Publishing Company, 1945.

Keach, Benjamin, Preaching from the types and Metaphors of the Bible, Grand Rapids, Michigan: Kregel Publications, 1972.

Marshall, A., The Interlinear Greek-English New Testament, Grand Rapids, Michigan: Zondervan Publishing House, 1972.

Moorehead, W. G., The Tabernacle, Grand Rapids, Michigan: Kregel Publications, 1966.

Mount, R. H., The Law Prophesied, Mansfield, Ohio: Mount Publications, 1966.

Newberry, Thomas, Types of Levitical Offerings, Bible Study Classics.

Olford, Stephen F., The Tabernacle: Camping with God, Neptune, New Jersey: Loizeaux Brothers, Inc., 1971.

Parker, Joseph, Preaching Through the Bible, 15 volumes, Grand Rapids, Michigan: Baker Book House, 1971.

Pfeiffer, Charles F., The Epistle to the Hebrews, Chicago, Illinois: Moody Press, 1962.

Ridout, Samuel, Lectures on the Tabernacle, New York, New York: Loizeaux Brothers, Inc., 1973.

Seiss, J. A., The Gospel in Leviticus, Grand Rapids, Michigan: Zondervan Publishing House.

Simpson, A. B., Christ in the Tabernacle, Harrisburg, Pennsylvania: Christian Publications Inc.

Slemming, Charles W., These are the Garments, Chicago, Illinois: Moody Press, 1955.

Soltau, Henry W., The Holy Vessels and Furniture, Grand Rapids, Michigan: Kregel Publications.

Stevens, Charles H., The Wilderness Journey, Chicago, Illinois: Moody Press, 1971.

Strong, James, Strong's Exhaustive Concordance, Grand Rapids, Michigan: AP and A. Publishing Company.

Tenney, Merrill C. and others, The Zondervan Pictorial Bible Dictionary, Grand Rapids, Michigan: Zondervan Publishing House, 1970.

Wilson, Walter Lewis, Wilson Dictionary of Bible Types, Grand Rapids, Michigan: W. B. Eerdman's Publishing Co., 1965.

www.ingramcontent.com/pod-product-compliance
Lightning Source LLC
LaVergne TN
LVHW091315080426
835510LV00007B/501